The Kingdom of God

Solomon Hailu, Ph.D.

Table of Contents

Chapter One

Origin of the Kingdom of God on Earth

God's government began on earth thousands of years ago when God placed Adam in charge of governing the earth. As God's appointed governor, Adam was bestowed with spiritual, moral, and intellectual capacity to effectively rule over every creation on earth. The Scripture says, God blessed them and said to them, "be fruitful and increase in number; fill the earth and subdue it. Rule over the fish in the sea and the birds in the sky and over every living creature that moves on the ground" (Genesis 1:28).

God never shared His administrative authority with any other creation. Even the angels were kept from ruling over God's creation. However, Adam's rule on earth was suspended because of his disobedience of God's command. Adam chose to listen to Satan's deception and lies. Subsequently, Satan took over man's authority of governing the earth in an illegal and illegitimate way.

It is important to note that God never put Satan as ruler of the earth. God is a good God who is never behind anything evil. It was Adam who ceded his authority to Satan. Even though Satan was able to takeover man's legitimate authority over earth through trickery, the kingdom of God continued to exist in Heaven, before time and throughout time forever. Therefore, the kingdom of God is timeless! David said, "Your kingdom is an everlasting kingdom, and your dominion endures through all generations" (Psalm 145:13). St. Peter reaffirmed that the kingdom of God is an everlasting kingdom (2 Peter 1:11).

The Lord Jesus Christ came to earth in human form to restore the lost kingdom of God to man's rule. Once his kingdom is established, nobody will take away again from the Lord Jesus Christ. "He will be great and will be called the Son of the Most High. The Lord God will give him the throne of his father David, and he will reign over Jacob's descendants forever; his kingdom will never end" (Luke 1:32-33).

The Lord Jesus came to restitute an extension of his Heavenly Kingdom upon earth. In the end, the kingdom of the world will have become the kingdom of our Lord and of his Messiah, and he will reign for ever and ever (Revelation 11:15). The kingdom of God is unshaken, but it shakes every other kingdom on earth. The Bible declares that "since we are receiving a kingdom that cannot be shaken, let us be thankful, and so worship God acceptably with reverence and awe" (Hebrews 12:28).

The Lord Jesus did not have greater mission than establishing the kingdom of God on earth. Therefore, he exclusively taught and preached about the Kingdom of God through parables and sermons.

The Lord Jesus Christ performed signs and wonders, including healing, casting out demons and miracles to reinforce his kingdom. However, his primary emphasis was not healing the sick, casting out demons and performing miracles. He performed those signs and wonders to confirm his coming kingdom on earth.

Undeniably, the miracles Jesus performed granted temporary relief to those who needed them. For example, thousands of people who were fed by Jesus in the desert became hungry again. Those who were delivered from the storm likely faced another storms. Those who were healed from sicknesses got sick again. Those who were raised from the dead had died again.

Nevertheless, the miracles were used as instruments to advance the kingdom of God and to demonstrate the power of Jesus as the Messiah, the Son of God, and that by believing we may have life in his name (John 20:30).

Chapter Two

Centrality of the Kingdom of God

The Lord Jesus Christ came to earth with the primary mission of establishing the kingdom of God on earth. Jesus never came to establish a charity organization, social institution, religious movement, or secular political system, but to establish God's kingdom government on earth.

Jesus inaugurated his incoming government on earth at his very first public sermon in his child province of Galilee. Jesus proclaimed that the "kingdom of God has come near" (Mark 1:15). From that time on Jesus invited all mankind to repent as a precondition to enter the kingdom of God. Jesus said, "Unless you repent, you too will all perish" (Luke 13:4).

Therefore, all it takes to enter the kingdom of God is to recognize our sins and sincerely repent. The Bible reassures us that if we confess our sins, "he is faithful and just and to forgive us our sins and purify us from all unrighteousness" (1 John 1:9). Jesus made repentance not as an option but an obligation to enter the kingdom of God. Since repentance is the gateway to the kingdom of God, we should do it. As the door is the only legitimate entry way into our house, so is repentance the only designated way to enter the kingdom of God.

Jesus continued to extend his call to repent to other cities. Jesus said, "I must preach the good news of the kingdom of God to the other towns as well; for I was sent for this purpose" (Luke 4:43). He traveled about from one town and village to another, proclaiming the good news of the kingdom of God (Luke 8:1).

The subject of kingdom continued to dominate Jesus' message to the last days of his ministry on earth. After his resurrection, Jesus appeared to his followers over a period of forty days and spoke about the kingdom of God (Acts 1:3). This clearly highlights the centrality of the kingdom of God in Christ's mission on earth.

Mandate to the Disciples

The Lord Jesus mandated his disciples to proclaim the kingdom of God as a matter of priority. He instructed them to declare the kingdom of God both collectively and individually. Jesus said to them, "As you go, proclaim the kingdom of heaven has come near" (Matthew 10:7).

The early apostles also preached the kingdom of God individually. The apostle Paul proclaimed the kingdom of God during his missionary works as recorded in the Book of Acts and in his epistles. For example, the Apostle Paul "entered the synagogue in Ephesus and spoke boldly there for three months, arguing persuasively for the kingdom of God" (Acts 19:8). At his farewell to the Ephesian Elders, he said, "Now I know that none of you among whom I have gone about preaching the kingdom will ever see me again" (Acts 20:25). Paul "proclaimed the kingdom of God—with all boldness and without hindrance" (Acts 28:31).

Paul's writings also placed significant emphasis on the kingdom of God. For example, he wrote to the Corinthian believers that "the kingdom of God is not a matter of talk, but of power" (1

Corinthians 4:20). He warned the Corinthians that "wrongdoers will not inherit the kingdom of God" (1 Corinthians 6:9). He explained the nature of the kingdom of God in his epistle to the Romans in which he said, "For the kingdom of God is not a matter of eating and drinking, but of righteousness, peace and joy in the Holy Spirit" (Romans 14:17).

Paul continued to emphasize his message on the kingdom of God in his letters to the other churches, as well. For example, in his letter to the Colossians, Paul wrote, "For he has rescued us from the dominion of darkness and brought us into the kingdom of the Son he loves" (Colossians 1:13). To the Thessalonian church, he wrote, "We encouraged, comforted, and implored each one of you to walk worthy of God, who calls you into His own kingdom and glory" (1Thessalonians 2:12). Paul further declared, "It is a clear evidence of God's righteous judgment that you will be counted worthy of God's kingdom, for which you also are suffering" (2 Thessalonians 1:5).

In his message to Timothy, Paul says, "I solemnly charge you in the presence of God and of Christ Jesus, who is to judge the living and the dead, and by his appearing and his kingdom" (2 Timothy 4:1). Paul also stated, "The Lord will rescue me from every evil work and will bring me safely into His heavenly kingdom. To him be the glory forever and ever! Amen" (2 Timothy 4:18).

The other apostles also preached the kingdom of God. The apostle Peter said, "Therefore, my brothers and sisters, make every effort to confirm your calling and election. For if you do these things, you will never stumble, and you will receive a rich welcome into the eternal kingdom of our Lord and Savior Jesus Christ" (2 Peter 1:10-11). The apostle James wrote, "Listen, my beloved brethren: has God not chosen the poor of this world to be rich in faith and heirs of the kingdom which he promised to those who love him (James 2.5).

The evangelist Philip proclaimed the kingdom of God to the people of Samaria. "Philip preached the things concerning the kingdom of God and the name of Jesus Christ, both men and women were baptized" (Acts 8:12).

Clearly, Jesus and his early disciples placed significant emphasis on the kingdom of God in all their teachings, preaching, and sermons. However, many contemporary Christian denominations have relegated the Lord Jesus' message of his heavenly government to the backburner of their pulpits.

It is quite common to hear contemporary churches place more emphasis on the preaching of other components of the Gospel, such as miracles, deliverance, money, resurrection, and healings other than the kingdom of God. Those pulpits put the cart before the horse. Although preaching on those subjects is important, they are not to diminish the central message of God's kingdom government.

The contemporary church has no greater mandate than to advance the kingdom of God. Therefore, all its teaching and preaching should primarily emphasize on the kingdom of God. The church that does not emphasize the message of the kingdom is not proclaiming the right message and, therefore, is missing Jesus' mandate of furthering the kingdom of God on earth.

Jesus is the Kingdom Message

At the center of the kingdom message is Christ himself. Jesus is not the messenger of the Kingdom of God; he personifies the message of the Kingdom of God. Jesus is not simply a messenger of salvation; he is the Savior himself. He is not just a messenger of healing; he is the Healer himself. He is not just a messenger of peace; he himself is our peace (Ephesians 2:14). Jesus is not just a messenger of truth; he is absolute truth itself. Jesus said, "I am the way and the truth and the life. No one comes to the Father except through me" (John 14:6). He is not just a messenger of the way to God; he is the way to the kingdom of God. He is the gatekeeper and the door to the kingdom of God. He is not just a messenger of a bread of life; he is the bread of life. As it is written: Jesus declared, "I am the bread of life. Whoever comes to me will never go hungry, and whoever believes in me will never be thirsty" (John 6:35).

Jesus is the message of the kingdom of God. If we take the message seriously, we will get the results of the message. Since Jesus is the central message of the kingdom, he should be exclusively exalted in his kingdom.

Jesus is king of the kingdom of God. There is no kingdom without a king, and there is no king without a kingdom. The kingdom should be built, maintained and run by the authority and power of the king. The word of the king should be a message and the main law of the land. There should not be any authority or law above the word of the king. Jesus is the one, perfect God. He is of the same substance as the Father and Holy Spirit. Jesus represented God among people. He expressed God in his divine character and holy living. Whoever saw Jesus saw God, for he was God in the flesh. God revealed himself to humanity through the person of Christ. There is no greater revelation in the Bible than Jesus himself. Jesus said, "These are the very Scriptures that testify about me" (John 5:39). Therefore, Jesus should be presented as the primary message of the Bible. Every book in the Bible talks about Jesus. In fact, Jesus was the only reason for the writing of the Bible. Other stories in the Bible were secondary to the main character—Jesus Christ!

Jesus was the complete message from God. Jesus was the only message of the Father God to humanity. A voice from heaven said, "This is my Son, whom I love; with him I am well pleased" (Matthew 3:17). The Father again said, "This is my Son, whom I have chosen; listen to him" (Luke 9:35). The Holy Spirit came to testify about Jesus. Jesus said, "When the Advocate comes, whom I will send to you from the Father—the Spirit of truth who goes out from the Father—he will testify about me (John 15:26). Angles announced the coming of Jesus to the world. The Holy Spirit revealed baby Jesus to Simon, the priest at the temple. "It had been revealed to him by the Holy Spirit that he would not die before he had seen the Lord's Messiah" (Luke

2:26). The angle announced "in the town of David a Savior has been born to you; he is the Messiah, the Lord" (Luke 2.11). The disciples exclusively preached Christ. In her first public ministry, Mary, mother of Jesus preached Jesus at the wedding. His mother said to the servants, "Do whatever he tells you" (John 2:5). She connected them with Jesus when what they hoped for ran out unexpectedly.

The apostles did not preach something else. They preached Christ. John said about Jesus: "That which was from the beginning, which we have heard, which we have seen with our eyes, which we have looked at and our hands have touched—this we proclaim concerning the Word of life" (1 John 1:1). John presented Jesus as his main message.

Jesus was the central message of the other apostles as well. For example, Paul devoted himself exclusively to preaching, testifying to the Jews that Jesus was the Messiah (Acts 18:5). Paul preached Christ and him crucified" (1 Corinthians 1:23). Paul declared "what we preach is not ourselves, but Jesus Christ as Lord" (2 Corinthians 4: 5). Paul wrote to the Ephesians, "Jesus Christ himself being the chief cornerstone, in whom the whole building, being fitted together, grows into a holy temple in the Lord, in whom you also are being built together for a dwelling place of God in the Spirit" (Ephesians 2:19-22). It was with boldness that Paul proclaimed this message regarding the Lord Jesus Christ (Acts 28:31).

The apostle Peter also preached on Christ exclusively. For example, at his first public preaching, which took place on the day of Pentecost. Peter devoted his entire message to explaining who Jesus is. He said,

> God has raised this Jesus to life, and we are all witnesses of it. Exalted to the right hand of God, he has received from the Father the promised Holy Spirit and has poured out what you now see and hear. God has made this Jesus, whom you crucified, both Lord and Messiah. When the people heard this, they were cut to the heart and said to Peter and the other apostles, "Brothers, what shall we do?" Peter replied, "Repent and be baptized, every one of you, in the name of

Jesus Christ for the forgiveness of
your sins. (Acts 2:32-38)

In his letter, Peter also emphasized on Jesus of being our cornerstone:

> As you come to him, the living Stone—
> rejected by humans but chosen by God and
> precious to him— you also, like living
> stones, are being built into a spiritual house
> to be a holy priesthood, offering spiritual
> sacrifices acceptable to God through Jesus
> Christ. For in Scripture it says: "See, I lay
> a stone in Zion, a chosen and precious
> cornerstone, and the one who trusts in him
> will never be put to shame." Now to you
> who believe, this stone is precious. But to
> those who do not believe, "The stone the
> builders rejected has become the
> cornerstone," and, "A stone that causes
> people to stumble and a rock that makes
> them fall." They stumble because they
> disobey the message—which is also what
> they were destined for (1 Peter 2:4-8).

Philip preached Christ to the Ethiopian eunuch. The Ethiopian asked Philip, "Tell me, please, who is the prophet talking about, himself or someone else?" Then Philip began with that very passage of Scripture and told him the good news about Jesus (Acts 8:34-35). The eunuch was saved.

When Jesus is preached, people get saved. The kingdom of God expands. For example, Philip preached Christ to the Samaritan people. Acts 8:5-8 presents the story of Philip traveling down to a city in Samaria and proclaiming the Messiah there. It reads:

> "When the crowds heard Philip and saw the signs he performed, they all paid close attention to what he said. For with shrieks, impure spirits came out of many, and many who were paralyzed or lame were healed. So there was great joy in that city."

We notice that when Jesus was preached in Samaria, many were saved and many signs, miracles, deliverances took place. People were filled with joy and peace.

Therefore, the person of Jesus must dominate the message of the contemporary church as a precondition to experience the same results of the early church. The church must declare that whoever "looks to the Son and believes in him shall have eternal life" (John 6:40).

The church must preach that Jesus is the resurrection and the life: "He who believes him will live, even though he dies; and whoever lives and believes in him will never die" (John 11:25-26). The church must preach that Jesus is the light of the world. He is the chief cornerstone and the savior of all humanity. Thus, it is clear the church must preoccupy itself with the core message of the kingdom—preaching and teaching about Jesus Christ and what he has done. Any other message does not lead to the Father (John 14:6). Salvation is only through faith in Jesus Chrsit. Whoever enters the kingdom through Jesus will enter the presence of God. There are many religions in the world, but there is only one way to Heaven. Jesus Christ is the only way, and he is the only message.

Chapter Three

The Kingdom vs Working of Miracles

The Lord Jesus' ministry has been widely recognized by various religious and political communities throughout history for performing marvelous miracles. For examples, Islam teaches Jesus was a miracle worker. The Jewish religious leaders of his day not only recognized him for performing miracles but were troubled by the numerous miracles Jesus performed. However, the assumption that Jesus came to earth just to perform miracles is a mistake!

Jesus was not only a miracle worker; he was the founder of the kingdom government of God on earth. The miracles were performed under the auspices of the kingdom government of God. In other words, the miracles Jesus performed were byproducts of the preaching and teaching of the kingdom of God. Thus, the miracles were not expected to outshine the more important and far greater mission of establishing Jesus' kingdom on earth.

This is not to say that the miracles Jesus performed were unnecessary. The miracles were vital not only to end human physical and spiritual infirmities but also to advance God's kingdom government on earth. The miracles by themselves were not an end; rather, they were signs that the kingdom of God is coming near. Jesus said, "If it is by the Spirit of God that I drive out demons, then the kingdom of God has come upon you" (Matt 12:28).

Normally, Jesus performed miracles after preaching the kingdom, not before. As Matthew 4:23 reads "Jesus went about all Galilee, teaching in synagogues, preaching the gospel of the kingdom, and healing all manner of sickness and disease among the people." This verse confirms that Jesus spoke of the kingdom before performing miracles. His kingdom message made the way for miracles to happen. Jesus pointed out that entering his kingdom is more important than receiving physical healings.

Jesus further emphasized the importance of the Kingdom of God over other things when he said, "Seek first his kingdom and his righteousness, and all these things will be given to you as well" (Matthew 6:33). The kingdom of God is more important than its benefits, such as healings and deliverance. Therefore, it is important to emphasize that the benefits of the kingdom must not come before the kingdom. The miracles are not as significant as the kingdom itself, for the kingdom of God is eternal while miracles are only temporary.

In fact, we position ourselves to receive miracles when we first seek the kingdom of God. Seeking miracles will not qualify us to enter the kingdom, but seeking the kingdom makes miracles occur. The Scriptures say Jesus "welcomed them and spoke to them about the kingdom of God, and healed those who needed healing" (Luke 9:11).

Jesus did not do any miracles until he preached the kingdom of God. Jesus made it clear that he did not cherish the crowds who came to see or experience miracles before seeking the kingdom of God. Indeed, he condemned those who simply sought miracles. The Bible says,

> Then some of the scribes and
> Pharisees answered him, saying,
> 'Teacher, we wish to see a sign from
> you.' But he answered them, 'An
> evil and adulterous generation seeks
> for a sign, but no sign will be given
> to it except the sign of the prophet
> Jonah' (Matthew 12:38–39).

Jesus rebuked them for seeking more miracles then him.

King Herod hoped to see Jesus performed miracles for him but Jesus refused.

> When Herod saw Jesus, he was
> greatly pleased, because for a long
> time he had been wanting to see him.
> From what he had heard about him,
> he hoped to see him perform a sign
> of some sort. He plied him with
> many questions, but Jesus gave him
> no answer (Luke. 23:8-9).

I have met many people who considered experiencing miracles as a precondition to entering the kingdom of God. Essentially, they do not wish to enter the kingdom of God unless their provisions are ensured in advance. For examples, the father of a sick child once said to a preacher, "I will follow Jesus if he only heals my daughter," but to the

24

man's dissatisfaction, the child was not healed after prayer. The man decided not to follow Jesus because his child did not receive healing. God does not answer such conditional prayers. He seeks for those who love and follow Him because He is God. God loves us unconditionally, and He expects us to return His love unconditionally.

Jesus does not commit himself to those who seek benefits more than himself. It is written,

> Now while he was in Jerusalem at the Passover Festival, many people saw the signs he was performing and believed in his name. But Jesus would not entrust himself to them, for he knew all people (John 2:23-24).

They were more interested in pursuing miracles than the miracle worker.

When Jesus offered his disciples an option to leave, Simon Peter answered him, "Lord, to whom shall we go? You have the words of eternal life. We have come to believe and to know that you are the Holy One of God" (John 6:68-69). Peter knew that eternal life is more important than signs, wonders, and miracles. Jesus warned his disciples not to be so concerned about perishable things, but to spend their energy "seeking the eternal life that the Son of Man can give" (John 6:27).

Jesus insisted that the recipients of his healing virtue should not tell the public about their miracles for the simple reason of preventing misunderstandings about his central mission, which was to establish the kingdom. Jesus commanded them not to tell anyone about their healings (Mark 7:36). When healings come before the kingdom, they are distractors. In the following story, Jesus tells the two healed blind men to keep the story of their healings a secret:

> As Jesus went on from there, two blind men followed him, calling out, "Have mercy on us, Son of David!" When he had gone indoors, the blind men came to him, and he asked them, "Do you believe that I am able to do this?" "Yes, Lord," they replied. Then he touched their eyes and said, "According to your faith let it be done to you"; and their sight was restored. Jesus warned them sternly, "See that no one knows about this." But they went out and

spread the news about him all over that region. (Matthew 9:27-31).

God's healing power is available within the kingdom. Jesus was upset with the Gentile woman for asking him for healing instead of seeking his kingdom first. Jesus replied, "It is not right to take the children's bread and toss it to the dogs" (Matthew 15:26). Jesus describing the woman as a dog did not mean he labeled her as less than human; instead, he wanted to convey that a hungry dog will normally run away once he gets his bone. The trouble with the woman was that she only wanted healing, not the kingdom.

Furthermore, Jesus had a way of keeping demonic spirits from revealing who he was in order to prevent them from distorting his mission. In Luke 4:35, he forcefully commanded demonic forces to be quiet and leave.

No message more powerfully frustrates the devil than that of the kingdom of God. The devil does not want to hear the kingdom message preached because it disrupts his presence in people's lives. When the kingdom of God arrives in life, the devil's power is completely erased in the person's life; thus, the devil is against the kingdom of God. He tries to distract humans from the message of the kingdom by all means possible because he knows that preaching the kingdom of God deserves him of his territory.

The kingdom of God comes only when it is preached. If the kingdom of God is not preached, it does not expand into new territories. However, when the kingdom of God is proclaimed, the power of God backs it up. Therefore, Jesus proclaimed the kingdom of God. He never proclaimed signs and wonders. He performed them to demonstrate the power of his kingdom.

In similar fashion, Jesus commanded his disciples to proclaim the kingdom of God first and then heal the sick, as the following quote shows:

> "As you go, proclaim this message: 'the kingdom of heaven has come near'. Heal the sick, raise the dead, cleanse those who have leprosy, drive out demons. Freely you have

received; freely give" (Matthew 10:7-8).

Healings and deliverance are the byproducts of preaching the kingdom. As the message of the kingdom proceeds, miracles follow. Physical healings are temporary. Even if we are healed physically or emotionally, it will not last forever. Our physical body will eventually be worn out. But the kingdom of God is eternal; therefore, we should concentrate on the eternal more than on the temporary. Knowing the power in the message of the kingdom of God, Jesus instructed the seventy-two to preach the kingdom of God. Jesus said to them, "When you enter a town and are welcomed, eat what is offered to you. Heal the sick who are there and tell them, 'The kingdom of God has come near to you'" (Luke 10:8-10). Later, it is written, "The seventy-two returned with joy and said, 'Lord, even the demons submit to us in your name" (Luke 10:17). However, Jesus did not seem to be impressed with their excitement of having dominion over the evil spirits, saying, "Do not rejoice that the spirits submit to you, but rejoice that your names are written in heaven" (Luke 10:20). In other words, Jesus told his disciples to rejoice more for their name is written in the book of life as citizen of the kingdom of God.

The key to defeat the enemy is simply to preach the Kingdom of God. When the authority of the Kingdom of God arrives, the devil loses his grip and flees. Undoubtedly, the church that preaches the kingdom of God faces more resistance from the enemy because that church inflicts serious damages on the kingdom of Satan. The devil knows it is the most dangerous church in town and he does all he can to stop it.

If you want to expand your ministry and have large crowds in your church, preach the kingdom of God. If you want to often see signs and wonders in your ministry, preach the kingdom of God. If you want people with physical, mental, and spiritual infirmities to return to their homes differently than they arrived, preach the kingdom of God.

If you preach about the kingdom of God like Jesus did, you will have the same results Jesus had. When Jesus preached the kingdom, demons were cast out and the sick were healed. When you preach the kingdom of God, the devil and disease depart from people's lives, just as in Jesus' days. If you want the devil to run from people, preach the kingdom of God. If you want to see more healings in your ministry, preach the kingdom of God.

The kingdom must be preached all the time. We need not dwell on miracles, signs, and wonders, miracles, money, deliverance from demons; we need to preach the kingdom of God. For example, the trouble with the Judas Iscariot was that he was stealing money from Jesus. Similarly, if a person values money more than God, things will not turn out well that person's life and ministry.

The message that places less emphasis on the kingdom of God is a different gospel than the gospel of Jesus Christ. Some churches and ministries are wasting their valuable time and God's money on their pulpits and TV screens selling what they call "sacred products," such as holy water, holy oil, holy bread, and other artifacts from the Holy Land instead of preaching the kingdom of God. Others are very active in fundraising and promoting social activities instead of preaching the kingdom of God. We did not receive the gospel of money. We received the gospel of the kingdom. The church and ministry that does not place the kingdom of God at the center of its message is not only weak and powerless but also dying.

The central message of the gospel should be the kingdom of God. Jesus said, "This gospel of the kingdom will be preached in the whole world as a testimony to all nations, and then the end will come" (Matthew 24:14). The gospel is the vehicle to expand the kingdom of God. Unsurprisingly, all of Jesus' prayers, parables, sermons, deliverances, healings, preaching, and teachings were exclusively centered on expanding the kingdom of God. Therefore, the church should follow the way of the Master in preaching the gospel of the kingdom of God.

Chapter Four

Establishing the Kingdom First

Jesus taught us to pray, "Your kingdom come, your will be done, on earth as it is in heaven. (Matthew 6:9-10). Jesus taught us to pray that God's kingdom would come before His will would be done on earth. Therefore, one must embrace the kingdom of God before God allows His will to be done in one's life. God must be sought after first before our physical or spiritual needs.

Obviously, God's kingdom government must be established before extending services to its people, which include providing daily bread, forgiveness of sins, and deliverance from the evil. It is the same with any government; it must first exist before it can deliver services to its subjects. Jesus knew that the kingdom of God must be established to maintain law and order in his kingdom. Law and order cannot be enforced without forming a government in the first place.

Every country on earth must first establish its government to provide its citizens with basic economic, social and security benefits. It is important that the earthly government not only exist symbolically, but it must also have a real political, military and legal authority to protect and serve its people.

The British philosopher and political thinker Thomas Hobbes said, "Life without government would be solitary, poor, nasty, brutish, and short." Can you imagine what would happen to us and our families if earthly governments should cease to exist even for a second? We would descend into a "state of nature," whereby the rule of the jungle takes over. The more powerful entity would dominate and controls the weak and feeble in this state.

I was once in a developing country when the president of that country resigned and fled. All government entities collapsed within a matter of hours. The same day, hooligans and dangerous criminals broke out of the prisons and started looting and destroying public and private properties by taking advantage of the power vacuum. The collapse of the government and its law enforcement mechanisms allowed complete chaos and lawlessness in the country.

Since a country without a government cannot provide the necessary services and security for its population, the best way to restore peace, safety, and security in the country is by reestablishing the government. The government must regain control of the country to ensure the safety and wellbeing of its people. Arguably, the government must be put in place before citizens can get access to their government-sponsored benefits.

However, rebuilding a government from scratch is a daunting task, perhaps taking decades, requiring a willingness from public servants and to commit the limited resources available to meet the challenges. The internal and external elements that benefited due to the absence of government will continue to fight the restoration of government. They will do everything possible to spoil the peace and stability of the people by maintaining the *status quo* until a stronger authority comes to destroy them. Once they are destroyed, the new government can be installed to restore normalcy to the country.

The coming of Jesus to earth can be viewed similarly to the above scenario. Jesus must first establish his government on earth before he can extend the necessary rights and privileges to his people. However, the task of establishing his kingdom was not an easy one. Jesus encountered fierce resistances and violent conflicts on many fronts. Jesus said, "The kingdom of heaven has been subjected to violence, and violent people have been raiding it" (Matthew 11:12). Jesus was referring to the opposition and threats to the coming of his kingdom by the religious and political leaders. For example, King Herod was searching to kill Jesus as a child (Matthew 2:13). Another time, a mob "drove him out of town, and took him to the brow of the hill on which the town was built, in order to throw him from a cliff" (Luke 4:29). The Jewish religious leaders did all they could to destroy Jesus and ultimately handed him over to the Romans to be put to death on the cross.

In the realm of the spirit as well, Jesus engaged in ultimate spiritual warfare against the ruler of the kingdom of darkness who then ruled the world. The reason the Son of God appeared was to destroy the devil's work. (1 John 3:8) The devil fought back to remain in authority. Satan began his counter-attack against Jesus at the onset of Christ's ministry. Indeed, the first incident in Jesus' ministry was a test by Satan. The tempter came to him and said, "If you are the Son of God, tell these stones to become bread" (Matt 4:3). Satan continued to tempt Jesus, taking him to the top of a mountain and telling Him to throw himself down. Satan also took Jesus to the top of another mountain and told him that He could have all the riches he beheld if he would bow down and worship him. Satan presented these tests to Jesus to keep him from taking the very first step towards establishing his kingdom. However, each time he was tempted by Satan, Jesus responded with the Word of God.

Satan used the same tactics on Jesus that he had employed to take authority from Adam. He had persuaded Eve by throwing doubts into her mind about God and His commands. The same serpent continued trying to trick Jesus, but the conversation ended abruptly when Jesus ordered Satan to go away from him (Matt 4:10). Apparently, Satan targeted Jesus' ministry at the earliest stage of his ministry—before he had picked his disciples or started His public ministry.

Nevertheless, Jesus continued to fight Satan and his cohorts to establish his kingdom on earth. Scripture tells that demonic forces cried out, "What do you want with us, Son of God? Have you come here to torture us before the appointed time?" (Matthew 8:29).

Jesus raised his own army and engaged them in battle with the forces of darkness. Luke 9:1 reads, "When Jesus had called the Twelve together, he gave them power and authority to drive out all demons." At another occasion, the seventy-two came back to report, "Lord, even the demons submit to us in your name" (Luke 10:17).

Before Jesus could establish the kingdom of God on earth, he first had to destroy the enemy of his kingdom. Jesus understood that he could not abolish Satan's rule of earth through a peaceful transfer of power; Jesus prepared to wage an all-out war against Satan. Jesus cast Satan down from heavenly places (Luke 10:18). He also went down to the darkest place to uproot the authority of Satan at its very root while he was buried for three days. The Bible declares, "Having disarmed the powers and authorities, he made a public spectacle of them, triumphing over them by the cross" (Colossians 2:15).

Jesus took the keys away from the devil and gave them back to his followers. Jesus said, "I have given you authority to trample on snakes and scorpions and to overcome all the power of the enemy; nothing will harm you" (Luke 17:19).

Once Jesus removed the stumbling-block from building his kingdom, he charged his children to expand the kingdom until his second return: "Do not be afraid, little flock, for your Father has been pleased to give you the kingdom: (Luke 12:32). The fierce fight with the forces of darkness will continue until the kingdom of God fully consummated at the Second Return of our Lord Jesus Christ.

Chapter Five

God's System of Government

Jesus came to establish a kingdom system of government, which is known as the kingdom of God (Matthew 4:30). A kingdom is a form of rule whereby the king holds the supreme authority over his land and people. In the kingdom form of government, the king has absolute administrative authority over every affair in his territory such as civilian, military and legal affairs. The king is judge; he is the law-giver; the king is sovereign. That means that his power is absolute and his decisions are final, binding, and uncontested. Isaiah 33:22 reads, "For the Lord is our judge, the Lord is our lawgiver, the Lord is our king; it is he who will save us."

Scripture confirms that the Lord Jesus Christ is the reigning king over the kingdom of God. The authority of the government of God "rests on his shoulders," and "he will reign over Jacob's descendants forever; his kingdom will never end" (Luke 1:33, Isaiah 9:6). Jesus himself confirmed that he was the king of his kingdom. When Jesus stood before the governor, and the governor questioned him, 'Are you the king of the Jews?' And Jesus said to him, 'It is as you say'" (Matthew 27:11-13).

Jesus is not a constitutional or nominal monarch. Whereas these monarchs do not assume active political power, often serving as the nominal head of state without an active role in the national politics and administration, Jesus is an absolute monarch. An example of a nominal ruler is the British royal family. The queen and her successor are only the symbolic head of state. Jesus, however, holds active administrative authority in His kingdom. He is the reigning king over his people and territory, and he is the commander-in-chief of his army. He oversees the physical, spiritual, and psychological needs of his people. He is the defender of his territory, and his rule shines in His kingdom forever.

The Kingdom of God is Not a Democracy

The kingdom of God is not a democratic system of government. The democratic political system is rule of the people, by the people, for the people. In a democratic system, the majority of the population decides who should assume the government office. In other words, the people decide who should govern them through elected representatives as prescribed by the Constitution, which is the main law of the land.

Under a democratic system, the government is subject to the people. The people have supreme authority over their government. The will of the people has priority in the democratic system of government. The people appoint public officials to work within various branches of government and to decide the power-relationships between the different branches of government. In the kingdom of God, however, God Himself is the highest authority, and His sovereignty does not rest on recognition from the people. He did not take power through democratic election. He is the Creator and

Sustainer of his creation. He rules with justice and righteousness.

The Kingdom of God is not Authoritarian

God's system of government is not an authoritarian system, where government authority is dependent on the strength of its military and intelligence services. Under an authoritarian regime, power is highly concentrated in the hand of a single individual.

As discussed above, democracy places the people above government. Authoritarian rule places governing authorities above the people. Authoritarian regimes restrict the freedoms of private enterprises, and they control the country's population by violating human rights and controlling its economy. In contrast to the officials elected in democracies, authoritarian rulers do not rule for limited time. The authoritarian system rule is depends not on popular legitimacy, but on coercive force by the political authorities. As we will see in the next section, the kingdom of God is not an authoritarian rule. King Jesus invites people to join his kingdom if they will to do. He rules with love, compassion, truth and justice.

There are several different types of authoritarian rule and governments on earth. The most commonly known authoritarian governments include 1. Autocratic, 2. Totalitarian, 3. Theocracy, and 4. Dictatorship.

Autocratic rule claims power through military means or divine appointment. It takes over foreign lands through military conquest. Some ancient examples of autocratic rule include the Greek Empire, Babylonian Empire, Egyptian Empire, Roman Empire, Ottoman Empire, precolonial African Empires, Latin American and Asian Empires.

Most European imperial rule was transformed to a constitutional monarchy. Under a constitutional monarchy, the monarch does not assume active political power. The monarch is but a nominal head of state. Japan, Belgium, the Nordic states, Great Britain, and other members of the commonwealth states exercise a constitutional system of monarchy where the monarch is limited to participate in national politics only in line with the constitution.

In a totalitarian system of government, a single party controls the government. The country is run by a single political party led by an all-powerful leader or a small committee of leaders. Other political parties are not allowed to compete for political power in the country. It is also known as a closed political system one which keeps opposing political groups from competing for power in the country. Individual rights and freedoms are restricted under a totalitarian system of government. Socialist and nationalist governments such as Nazism, Fascism, and radical Islamist regimes are totalitarian systems of government.

The theocratic system of government is a rule by a religious leader. The theocrat is the highest political and religious figure in the country. State and its religion are not separate. The theocrat makes political decisions based on religious inspiration or revelations. A good example of such a kind of government is what came into power in Iran after the 1979 Islamic Revolution, which overthrew the pro-western Shah's kingdom of Iran. Since the revolution, Iran has been ruled by a supreme leader called the Ayatollah, which means a high-ranking Shiite Muslim leader.

The Ayatollah assumes the highest political authority in matters of government. All elected government officials, including the president, parliament, and judicial system are under the supreme authority of the Ayatollah. In other words, the Ayatollah has absolute power over all government mechanisms. As the highest political authority in the land, any political or legal decision made by the Ayatollah are final and binding. We also see theocracy in places where autocratic rulers appoint themselves the head of both the state and its religion.

Dictatorship is rule by an individual or oligarchies (a group of people) who have amassed political power through military force or other subversive ways. The dictator may rule with or without the label of a political party; however, the real power is more concentrated in the hands of a ruler than the political party. The dictator rules with an iron fist. That means dictator personally controls subjects through propaganda of fear and intimidation. A dictator rules the country through military power. Law enforcement and other state mechanisms, including the army and police, serve the interest of the dictator more than the interest of the wider public. News media is typically state-owned or controlled by groups connected with the ruling regime who largely serve to terrorize the population. Dictatorship is characterized by widespread repression of civil and political rights. There is no independent judiciary. Justices are patron of the regime.

King Jesus vs Earthly Kings

Unlike the earthly authoritarian rulers, King Jesus is the defender of his people. He is the only savior king in the world who puts his life on the line for his people. Jesus said of himself, "I am the good shepherd: the good shepherd giveth his life for the sheep" (John 10:11). King Jesus came to give his life for others (Matthew 20:28). "For even the son of man did not come to be served, but to serve, and to give his life as a ransom for many" (Mark 10:45). Jesus was afflicted, humiliated, bruised, and killed to open his kingdom to humanity. The Lord Jesus opened his kingdom of peace and joy to whoever wants to enter it.

King Jesus protects and provides for his people. He is an absolute sovereign ruler who meets the needs of his people in abundance. The psalmist sings about the Lord's provision and protection in the following passage:

> The Lord is my shepherd, I lack nothing. He makes me lie down in green pastures, he leads me beside quiet waters, he refreshes my soul. He guides me along the right paths for his name's sake. Even though I walk through the darkest valley, I will fear no evil, for you are with me; your rod and your staff, they comfort me. You prepare a table before me in the presence of my enemies. You anoint my head with

oil; my cup overflows. Surely your goodness and love will follow me all the days of my life, and I will dwell in the house of the Lord forever (Psalm 23).

Jesus never stands behind his army during the battles. His sheep follow him (John 10:27). He leads his army to victory. Earthly rulers are the last to go to war, whereas citizens are forced at the frontlines to die to protect the king and royal families, who might even leave the country when a foreign enemy invades. Jesus said, "Rulers of the Gentiles lord it over the people, and their high officials exercise authority over them" (Matthew 20:25). Unlike the earthly rulers, Jesus never forces his government on the people. Jesus invites people to join his kingdom on a voluntary basis, saying, "Come to me, all of you who are weary and carry heavy burdens, and I will give you rest" (Matthew 11:28).

Jesus is a gentle ruler who does not impose his own welfare on the people. He said, "Here I am! I stand at the door and knock. If anyone hears my voice and opens the door, I will come in and eat with that person, and they with me" (Revelation 3:20). Jesus is not a controlling ruler. He gave his followers the option to stop following him anytime they wished. John 6:66-69 says many of his disciples turned back and no longer followed him. Jesus asked his twelve disciples, "You do not want to leave too, do you?" Simon Peter was the one to answer Jesus, saying, "Lord, to whom shall we go? You have the words of eternal life. We have come to believe and to know that you are the Holy One of God."

Jesus is more accessible than earthly rulers. He was spending his time with the poor, the rejected and the downtrodden. He ate meals with sinners, tax collectors, prostitutes, and hated ones. Jesus visited the poor, broken-hearted, and the destitute. He travelled to heal the sick and to raise the dead. Earthly rulers either beat or imprison those who lingered at their palaces for fear of their own security. Even worse, they kill their people to stay in power. Jesus died to save his people. Jesus shares his throne with his people (Matthew 19:28). The Bible says we reign with him. We are seated on the right hand of God (on His throne) with Christ. Luke 12:32 reads, "Do not be afraid, little flock, for your Father has been pleased to give you the kingdom."

The kingdom of God belongs to the King and his people, whereas earthly kingdoms belong to their king and the royal family. Earthly kings impose taxes on their people, while they and their family are exempt from paying. In the Gospel of Matthew, Jesus asked "From whom do the kings of the earth collect duty and taxes—from their own children or from others?" It was Peter who answered, "From others." Jesus then replied, "Then the children are exempt" (Matthew 17:25-26). Earthly kings live above the law, but Jesus obeyed the law. Jesus himself paid taxes and paid people's debt for sin. Jesus obeyed the law.

Jesus is a king who protects his people. He said to his captors, "I told you that I am he. If you are looking for me, then let these men go" (John 18:8). King Jesus saves at no cost to sinners. He delivers for free. He heals without charge. He does not judge what he sees. King Jesus loves his people more than himself. He knows each citizen by name. He is always victorious over the devil and death, and he always forgives. King Jesus is a servant King; he is not an authoritarian ruler.

Jesus is the everlasting king. His throne is for eternity. He is Alpha and Omega. Earthly rulers die, but Jesus died and resurrected. Once resurrected, Jesus became alive forevermore. He is the same yesterday, today, and forever. He is the only person who resurrected himself from the dead in all human history. Many have been raised from the dead, but did not resurrect. For example, Jesus raised Lazarus from death, but he did not resurrect him to live eternally in that body! Lazarus died again after a while, because he was only raised from the dead, not resurrected as was Jesus. Jesus did not die a second time because he was resurrected. Jesus is the only king who was actually resurrected. A person who is resurrected cannot die again. Jesus said, "I am the resurrection and the life. He who believes in me will live, even though he dies; and whoever lives by believing in me will never die" (John 11:25-26). Whoever believes in Jesus will be resurrected and never die again. Jesus has the ultimate say over death!

Romans 6:8-9 says, "Now if we died with Christ, we believe that we will also live with him. For we know that since Christ was raised from the dead, he cannot die again; death no longer has mastery over him." Jesus is the only king who has authority over everything in heaven and earth. In Matthew 28:18 Jesus says, "All authority in heaven and on earth has been given to me." Every authority submits to Jesus. He in control of every situation. Jesus defeated all his enemies; he never lost a battle. Even in his death, he won the battle. Earthly kings lost battles. They were either killed, surrender, or exiled. Jesus is the all-time winner; he is the everlasting king. His government has no end. He is the absolute-sovereign king.

Chapter Six

Attributes of the Kingdom of God

The kingdom of God has four fundamental attributes. The first is that the kingdom of God has a well-defined territory. Territory refers to the physical existence of the kingdom of God. John foresaw that the kingdom of God would have its own land: "I saw the Holy City, the new Jerusalem, coming down out of heaven from God, prepared as a bride beautifully dressed for her husband" (Revelation 21:2). The apostle Peter also confirmed that the kingdom of God will have physical existence: "But in keeping with his promise we are looking forward to a new heaven and a new earth, where righteousness dwells" (2 Peter 3:13).

The kingdom of God has well-defined boundaries.

> In his revelation, John saw in the kingdom of God a city foursquare with the length as large as its breadth. He measured the city with a reed, twelve thousand furlongs. The length and the breadth and the height of it are equal. And he measured the

wall thereof, an hundred and forty and four cubits, according to the measure of a man, that is, of the angel" (Revelation 21:16-17).

The second attribute of the kingdom of God is population or subjects. Kingdoms do not exist without subjects. A kingdom without a population is like Antarctica. No people live there—only penguins!

John said,

"After this I looked, and there before me was a great multitude that no one could count, from every nation, tribe, people and language, standing before the throne and before the Lamb. They were wearing white robes and were holding palm branches in their hands" (Revelation 7:9).

Apostle Peter also describes the population of the kingdom of God in his epistle:

"But you are a chosen people, a royal priesthood, a holy nation, God's special possession, that you may declare the praises of him who called you out of darkness into his wonderful light" (1 Peter 2:9).

The citizenship of the kingdom of God is the most precious and prestigious citizenship in the universe. The citizenship in the kingdom of God is imperishable. Jesus placed a condition to be admitted to the citizenship of the kingdom of God, and that is to be born again. Jesus said, "Very truly I tell you, no one can see the kingdom of God unless they are born again" (John 3:3). Jesus explained that the second birth is not biological or physical, but spiritual. He said, "Flesh gives birth to flesh, but the Spirit gives birth to spirit" (John 3:6). The apostle Paul made it clear that flesh and blood cannot inherit the kingdom of God nor does the perishable inherit the imperishable (1 Corinthians 15:50).

The new birth is triggered by the Holy Spirit who brings internal transformation of our heart and mind. Our old sinful nature will be nullified if we sincerely repent and believe that God forgives and forgets our sins through the washing by the blood of the Lord Jesus Christ and gives as the privilege of inheriting the kingdom of God.

The third attribute of the kingdom of God is government. Government is the highest political, legal, and administrative authority within a state which makes and enforces laws to protect and extend its benefits to the people of the kingdom. Even though the government is the highest authority in God's kingdom, it is not the kingdom itself. Kingdom and government are two distinct entities. Kingdom is a much larger and broader institution than government. Government is one of the features within the kingdom. In the kingdom of God, King Jesus is the chief officer. He is not a kingdom himself; rather, he runs the daily affairs of his kingdom as the highest government authority of the kingdom of God.

The fourth attribute of the kingdom of God is its sovereignty. Sovereignty means having recognition. Earthly ruling systems enjoy some degree of sovereignty or recognition from their citizens for meeting the basic needs of the people. Some earthly rules enjoy greater recognition than others for better serving their citizens. Other earthly rules, however, experience negative recognition from their people for providing lower levels of service. The more the sovereignty fails to meet the political, social, and economic needs of their citizens, the less recognition they receive.

Rulers with negative recognition maintain their *status quo* not on popular support but on the military power or external support. Their political power may come to an end in the face of growing unpopularity and sudden withdrawal of external support. For example, many governments in developing countries collapsed when the former Soviet Union suspended its economic and military support because of its own internal troubles. Those countries' sovereignty was dependent on the support of an external power. They did not encounter recognition from their subject as much as they had from the foreign power. Indeed, many great earthly empires in history quickly disappeared because they lacked internal and external sovereignty. The great Roman, Greek, Persian, and British Empires are examples of established structures which collapsed due to a lack of sovereignty.

Countries may differ from each other in the size of population, economy, territory, military power, culture, and political system. For example, Russia has the largest territory in the world; the United States has the biggest economy in the world; China is the most populous country in the world. However, despite smaller population and territory, and weaker economies, other countries still maintain equal external sovereignty in the international system. The United Nations Charter declares that every country is equal despite differences in their geographical, economic, and population size. All of them have diplomatic representation and their flags are at the United Nations headquarters in New York City and Geneva. All counties enjoy equal recognition at the international level; however, not all of them enjoy equal internal recognition by the people they govern. Some counties have a comparatively lower levels of internal recognition than others by their own people because they fail to provide the basic services to their citizens.

Countries with a low level of recognition are known as "failed states." The so-called failed state index provides an assessment of each country in the world based on various internal conditions to determine the level of recognition by their people. Even the so-called stable countries with relatively higher internal recognition do not enjoy full internal sovereignty from their citizens because they are not capable of meeting some of the critical needs of their population. For example, the United States, with both the largest economy and strongest militarily in the world, fails to provide free health care and education opportunities to its own citizens. Therefore, the United States is not listed at or near the top on the listed of countries which provide a higher living standard for their citizens.

God's kingdom exercises an absolute sovereignty in its own right. Unlike earthly kingdoms, God's kingdom is not dependent on recognition from its population; its sovereignty is dependent on the authority of God Himself. Jesus declared, "All authority is given to me in heaven and on earth" (Matthew 28:18). Human, natural, and spiritual authorities are subjected to the authority of our Lord Jesus Christ. For example, the apostle Paul reminded human masters to treat their slaves humanely, saying, "Do not threaten them, since you know that he who is both their Master and yours is in heaven. There is no favoritism with him" (Ephesians 6:9).

Jesus demonstrated his authority over nature on a number of occasions, such as in Matthew 8:23-27: "Jesus got up and rebuked the winds and the waves, and it was completely calm. The men were amazed and asked, "What kind of man is this? Even the winds and the waves obey him!"

Jesus has authority over the spirit realm, as well. For example, he has victory over physical death. He raised several people from the dead. The story of Lazarus is found in John 11:43-44: "Jesus called in a loud voice, 'Lazarus, come out!' The dead man came out, his hands and feet wrapped with strips of linen, and a cloth around his face. Jesus said to them, "Take off the grave clothes and let him go."

Jesus is seated at the right hand of God in the heavenly realms, "far above all rule and authority, power and dominion, and every name that is invoked, not only in the present age but also in the one to come" (Ephesians 1:20-21). The devil and his subordinates were subdued by the mighty authority of Jesus. In Matthew 8:29, demons shouted to Jesus, "What do you want with us, Son of God? Have you come here to torture us before the appointed time?"

God's sovereignty is uncontested throughout the universe. He is Adonai, meaning sovereign king, absolute and immortal ruler. His sovereignty covers every part of the universe. He fills the whole heaven and earth (Jeremiah 23:24). His sovereignty extends in hell as well as in heaven. He can do whatever he wants; He is God Almighty. The Psalmist declares God's sovereign authority in the following words: "The Lord does whatever pleases him, in the heavens and on the earth, in the seas and all their depths" (Psalm 135:6). God "causes his sun to rise on the evil and the good, and sends rain on the righteous and the unrighteous" (Matthew 5:45). He can sustain and guide all his creation (1 Samuel 2:6-7). God "has brought down rulers from their thrones but has lifted up the humble" (Luke 1:52).

God's sovereignty not only extends everywhere, but He is also able to grant His people abundance in every area of life. The Psalmist expressed his satisfaction with the Lord:

> Praise the Lord, my soul, and forget not all his benefits—who forgives all your sins and heals all your diseases, who redeems your life from the pit and crowns you with love and compassion, who satisfies your desires with good things so that your youth is renewed like the eagle's" (Psalm 103:2-5).

The Lord Jesus reaffirmed that God will provide the necessary provision and protection if we put our trust in Him. The Lord Jesus said,

> Therefore I tell you, do not worry about your life, what you will eat or

drink; or about your body, what you will wear. Is not life more than food, and the body more than clothes? Look at the birds of the air; they do not sow or reap or store away in barns, and yet your heavenly Father feeds them. Are you not much more valuable than they? Can any one of you by worrying add a single hour to your life? And why do you worry about clothes? See how the flowers of the field grow. They do not labor or spin. Yet I tell you that not even Solomon in all his splendor was dressed like one of these. If that is how God clothes the grass of the field, which is here today and tomorrow is thrown into the fire, will he not much more clothe you—you of little faith? So do not worry, saying, "What shall we eat?" or "What shall we drink?" or "What shall we wear?" For the pagans run after all these things, and your heavenly Father knows that you need them. But seek first his kingdom and his righteousness, and all these things will be given to you as well. Therefore do not worry about tomorrow, for tomorrow will worry about itself. Each day has enough trouble of its own (Matthew 6:25-34).

Chapter Seven

The Kingdom of God First

Jesus said, "But seek first his kingdom" (Matthew 6:33). To seek first His kingdom means several things.

1. It means to establish a relationship with God. Jesus emphasized that our relationship we may have with God is more important than any relationship in the world. The kingdom of God is the place where the relationship between God and His people is established.

The kingdom of God is not a religious institution. It is a place of reunion between humanity and Father God. If we are in a right relationship with God, the rest will go well in our life. Having a right relationship does not cause us to lose out on things; rather, having a right relationship with God is the best way of gaining other things. A person who puts his needs before God is not in a right relationship with God. If you have the kingdom, you have the rest added onto you (Matthew 6:33). Therefore, to prosper in all areas of life, one should not just seek material prosperity; instead pursue having a good relationship with God first. The Bible asks,

> Without him, who can eat or find enjoyment? To the person who pleases him, God gives wisdom, knowledge, and happiness, but to the sinner he gives the task of gathering and storing up wealth to hand it over to the one who pleases God. This too is meaningless, a chasing after the wind (Ecclesiastes 2:25-26).

Even if we achieve success without God, we will not enjoy it. I have known many so-called "accomplished" people in the business, entertainment, academic, and professional world, whose lives are in a complete disaster. I once met a young, overachieving woman on a flight to Chicago. She told me that she had just retired from her career at the age of thirty-nine. She had a tremendous success in her career. She made all her money the right way, but she had to retire because she lost joy in all her achievements. I asked her if she had a relationship with God. She answered,

"No." I told her it is never too late to begin a relationship with him. She tearfully accepted Jesus Christ as her Lord and Savior and began a new and exciting relationship with God. I could tell that the Spirit of the Lord came upon her dry and empty life that very moment.

It is more pleasing to have small things with God than to have the wealth of the world without Him. In Luke 15:8-31, Jesus provides a parable directed at those who had run away from the kingdom of God. In the parable, Jesus told about a father and his two sons. The younger son decided to take his portion from his father's estate and waste it in a far-away country. After incredible sufferings which involved starvation, homelessness and nakedness, he decided to go back to his father to live as one of his servants. However, the father restored his sonship again. Jesus wanted to convey a message that the moment we distance ourselves from the kingdom of God, the worst situations get their grip on our life. Obviously, the lost son wouldn't have had to suffer such a great deal had he not run away from his father's estate. In the same way, there are countless Christians who run away from the kingdom of God and suffer spiritually, physically, and mentally. Some are unable to return to the arms of God; other contract incurable diseases and die prematurely; some serve time in jail or become homeless or face unexpected pregnancy out of wedlock; others return to the bosom of the father God after they had sustained trauma from violence or drug abuse and could not break free.

2. To seek God kingdom first means to trust in God as the source of everything we need. We put God first not because of what he has done for us, but because of who He is. God is not a means to an end; He is an end in himself. God should not be used as a tool to get something; He must be the one sought after if we are to achieve our desires. When we meet God, our needs will be met. Without God, we cannot reach our goal, for God is the ultimate goal. No matter what happens, He is our God. As is written in Exodus 20:3, "You shall have no other

gods before me." In the story of Shadrach, Meshach, and Abednego, the three Hebrew boys said to King Nebuchadnezzar,

> If we are thrown into the blazing furnace, the God we serve is able to deliver us from it, and he will deliver us from Your Majesty's hand. but even if he doesn't, we want to make it clear to you, Your Majesty, that we will never serve your gods or worship the gold statue you have set up (Daniel 3:17-18).

We should not trust God conditionally. God is our provider. When you seek Him first, He guides you through decisions you must make. He can bless you with far more than what money can get you. He can provide opportunities, such as education, a career, or medical service that money cannot get you. I earned my Bachelors, Masters, and PhD without any cost. Someone asked if I belonged to a royal family or was born into wealth because I attended such a prestigious university. My answer to them was, "Yes." My heavenly Father owns everything. Diamond, gold and silver belong to him. How many of us have received a multimillion dollar medical treatment without paying a cent because of God's intervention? How many of us live in the most affluent communities because God opened doors for us? How many of us landed a dream job because of God's favor?

I remember when I arrived in the United States from South Africa in 2002 on my first academic trip. I had a limited-purpose visa and a limited time to stay in the country, but the Lord intervened in unexpected way. During an academic conference, three American professors came to me and offered me a visiting professorship position at their university. After I accepted the offer, they processed the extension of my visa without any cost to me. I was surprised by the offer, as a young and inexperienced professor. Only the favor of the Lord could open such a marvelous opportunity.

If you put God first, you position yourself to receive His blessing. If you put Him first, He will also put you first, and no obstacle will stop him from coming to you. The least in the kingdom of God is more privileged than the most powerful person on earth; everybody is first class in the kingdom of God. David reflected on this in his songs, saying that God's goodness and mercy would follow him for the rest of his life (Psalm 23:6). Even David made mistakes, but God's mercy brought him back into the line of blessing.

3. To seek first the kingdom of God means to fix our eyes on Jesus who is the king of the kingdom of God. Do you want the best in life? Put Jesus first; He will take care of you like nobody else—not only on this earth, but after their life. Even if things may seem wrong today, never lose your faith in Him. He will bless you. He cannot be beaten by some wealthy tycoons or heavy-weight politicians. He is the best. He will make you first when you surrender all your desires to him. God will not give you negative results for trusting in Him. He will make you the head and not the tail in all you do by putting your trust in Him.

4. To seek the kingdom of God first means to put God before your own self-interest. Therefore, we need to cut out anything that displeases the

Lord, whether that be our own fleshly desires or our love of the world. Offer your body as a living sacrifice (Romans 12:1). Jesus said,

> If your hand causes you to stumble, cut it off. It is better for you to enter life maimed than with two hands to go into hell, where the fire never goes out. And if your foot causes you to stumble, cut it off. It is better for you to enter life crippled than to have two feet and be thrown into hell. And if your eye causes you to stumble, pluck it out. It is better for you to enter the kingdom of God with one eye than to have two eyes and be thrown into hell (Mark 9:43-48).

Anything that is not in the service of the kingdom of God must be removed from our life. Some of the things we lust after with our eyes must be removed. Some of the things we reach out to with our hands must be removed. Some of the places we go must be removed.

5. To seek the kingdom of God first means to obey His word and trust in the promises of His word. As it is written in James 1:22, "Do not merely

listen to the world, and so deceive yourself. Do what it says." We must put God in the first place in our actions, not merely words. Children who only listen to their parents without doing what they say will face serious consequences.

6. To seek the kingdom of God first means to "Love the Lord your God with all your heart and with all your soul and with all your strength and with all your mind" (Luke 10:27). It means to love Him more than anything you need in your life such as family, food, money, material world, or good of the world itself. Jesus said, "Anyone who loves his life will lose it, while anyone who hates their life in this world will keep it for eternal life" (John 12:25). When you take matters into your own hands, you will become poor, sick, and live a short life. The Bible says, "Every good and perfect gift is from above, coming down from the Father of the heavenly lights, who does not change like shifting shadows" (James 1:17). Therefore, do not go your own way.

To love God means that He is more than money. In Ecclesiastes, Solomon writes, "Whoever loves money never has enough; whoever loves wealth is never satisfied with their income. This too is meaningless" (Ecclesiastes 5:10). Jesus explained, "No one can serve two masters. Either you will hate the one and love the other, or you will be devoted to the one and despise the other. You cannot serve both God and money" (Matthew 6:24). Ministers who have money on their mind never succeed. God sometimes takes money out of our life and sees if we will still trust Him.

To love God first means He is more to us than the world's material wealth, our love of sports, entertainment, or business. A man can keep himself from entering the kingdom of God on account of business. In Luke 14:19, Jesus presents the parable of the Great Banquet, in which one man says, "'I have just bought five yoke of oxen, and I'm on my way to try them out. Please excuse me.'" Jesus also remarked that it is "easier for a camel to go through the eye of a needle than for someone who is rich to enter the kingdom of God" (Matthew 19:24). We also read that

> A man runs up to Jesus as asks what he must do to enter the kingdom of God. Jesus replies, "Go, sell everything you have and give to the poor, and you will have treasure in heaven. Then come, follow me." The passage continues, "At this the man's face fell. He went away sad, because he had great wealth. Jesus looked around and said to his disciples, 'How hard it is for the rich to enter the kingdom of God!'" (Mark 10:17-25).

To love God first means to love Him more than our family, friends or social life. If you love your social life or your marriage more than God, you are in a wrong relationship with God. In the Parable of the Great Banquet, another man responded, "I just got married, so I can't come" (Luke 14:20). Jesus said, "Anyone who loves their father or mother more than me is not worthy of me; anyone who loves their son or daughter more than me is not worthy of me" (Matthew 10:37). Luke 9:59-62 gives us the following account:

Another disciple said, "Lord, first let me go and bury my father." Jesus said to him, "Let the dead bury their own dead, but you go and proclaim the kingdom of God." Still another said, "I will follow you, Lord; but first let me go back and say goodbye to my family." Jesus replied, "No one who puts a hand to the plow and looks back is fit for service in the kingdom of God."

John and his brother James left their father and their business of fishing to follow Jesus. I have known some friends who love God and their friends and want to keep both on the same level of affection; however, it is not possible to maintain equal love for God and one's friends. You either love God more than your friends or vice versa.

I once read a story about a renowned preacher who went to visit his cousin between his services. Forty-five minutes into the time with his cousin, the Spirit of the Lord said to him, "you have had enough time with your cousin, I need to spend time with you before the next service." However, the preacher ignored the voice and stayed longer with his cousin. He then went to the service from his cousin's house, and the usual presence of the Lord was not there. He was scared, embarrassed, and shocked that the presence of the Lord was not there to help the people. Even though the preacher cried and pleaded for the Lord to show up, it was to no avail. People who traveled thousands of miles and those who came on wheelchairs and stretchers went back disappointed. This was all due to the man of God spending more time with his family than with God. After the service ended with such dryness, he ran to his hotel room and asked the Lord what went wrong. The Lord answered him, "I told you to return to the hotel earlier, but you ignored me." The preacher apologized to the Lord and never did that again.

We servants of God should be aware that spending more time with the Lord is the key in success in the Lord's service. The more time we spend with God, the more we receive from him. The more we spend time with people, the less we have of God. Serving God costs everything but not without reward. Jesus told his disciples, "Truly I tell you, no one who has left home or wife or brothers or sisters or parents or children for the sake of the kingdom of God will fail to receive many times as much in this age, and in the age to come eternal life" (Luke 18:29-30).

7. To seek the kingdom of God first means do the will of God. Jesus said, "My food is to do the will of him who sent me and to finish his work" (John 4:34). Jesus prayed, "Your will be done on earth" (Matthew 6:10). The will of God must come before any other business endeavors. James wrote,

> "Why, you do not even know what will happen tomorrow. What is your life? You are a mist that appears for a little while and then vanishes. Instead, you ought to say, 'If it is the Lord's will, we will live and do this or that'" (James 4:13-15).

If you put God first in your business or professional endeavors, your business and career will be more secure. The devil will not be able to steal from you. He won't be able to kill or destroy you.

8. To seek the kingdom of God first means God should come before earthly citizenship,

identity, race, religion, culture or tradition. You cannot claim to love God when you discriminate against fellow humans based on cultural, racial, religious, political, or other backgrounds. Jesus accused the Pharisees of caring more about their culture and tradition than about entering the kingdom of God. Jesus was widely criticized by both Jews and Samaritans for violating ethnic, gender, and moral barriers during his conversation with the Samaritan woman. Mark, Matthew, and Luke commonly document that Jesus associated himself with socially-misfit women, whether Jews or non-Jews. For example, in Matthew 15:22-28 and Mark 7:24-30, Jesus heals a daughter of a Canaanite woman. In Luke 7:1-10, Jesus healed the centurion's slave girl. The Gospel of John also documents these claims.

Jesus dismantled all sorts of barriers. He removed the barrier between heaven and earth as well as racial, class, and economic barriers in humanity. As disciples of Christ, we ought to follow his example in reconciling people with God and making peace between people in the face of the widening political, economic, social (ethnic and gender), and spiritual divides among the people of his day. For example, the Samaritan woman told Jesus that He violated the Jewish tradition of a men talking to a woman unless they were family members. John 4:9 reads: "The Samaritan woman said to him, 'You are a Jew and I am a Samaritan woman. How can you ask me for a drink?' (for Jews do not associate with Samaritans.)"

Clearly, Jesus violated the Jewish tradition which prohibited cross-gender conversation. According to Jewish sages, Jewish men were to avoid unnecessary conversation with women. In early Judaism, Jewish men would try to avoid contact with Samaritan women, who were considered unclean. The Samaritan woman questioned Jesus: "You are a Jew and I am a Samaritan woman,. How can you ask me for a drink?" (John: 4.9).

However, it was more important for Jesus to extend his message of redemption to the Samaritans beyond Jewish cultural and religious boundaries. Jesus' conversation with the Samaritan woman marked the beginning of peaceful relations between the Christian, Jewish and Samaritan peoples. The conversation with Jesus and subsequent conversations with the people of Samaria set a precedent for Philip to preach to the Samaritans. As a disciple of Jesus, we need to imitate Christ, who loves all alike and treats everyone equally.

Chapter Eight

Kingdom Benefits

Earthly governments give priority to thier citizens in terms of access to political, economic and social services such as education, health care, employment, safe water, electricity, the right to vote, so on. Some government jobs require citizenship as a precondition to be considered for a position. For example, most of the US government jobs require that the applicant be a US citizen.

The citizens of other countries immigrate to the so-called developed countries in search of better living conditions or to flee political or religious persecution in their country of origin. They take every risk to access privileges in the developed countries by crossing vast deserts and rough oceans through illegal means without food and water for weeks. Some lose their families or even their lives along the way; others sell their property or spend the accumulated wealth to pay fees required to immigrate to the affluent parts of the world. Others take out loans with a high interest in hope of paying it back after they get to their destination.

In like manner, one must become a citizen of the kingdom of God to qualify for its benefits. Without becoming a citizen of the kingdom of God, one cannot get access to its benefits. The Bible says we are the citizens of heaven and the people of God (Philippians 3:20, 1 Peter 2:10). The citizens of Heaven are granted exceptional privileges, which come as part of their citizenship rights.

However, to accept the citizenship benefits of the kingdom of God, one must become a child through spiritual birth from God. The Scripture says,

> "to all who received him, to those who believed in his name, he gave the right to become children of God — children born not of natural descent, nor of human decision or a husband's will, but born of God" (John 1:12-13).

Our fellow human nature does not qualify us to enter the kingdom of God. Rather, God made a new way for us to enter his kingdom. He sent his son Jesus Christ to lead us into the kingdom of God by giving his life for our redemption. Although God offers his salvation free of charge, nevertheless, no one can enter the kingdom of God without a cost. Jesus said that the kingdom of God is like a person who found hidden treasure and sold everything he had to purchase the treasure (Matthew 13:44). The story of Jesus and the wealthy young man exemplifies this message:

> Just then a man came up to Jesus and asked, "Teacher, what good thing must I do to get eternal life?" "Why do you ask me about what is good?" Jesus replied. "There is only one who is good. If you want to enter life, keep the commandments." "Which ones?" he inquired. Jesus replied, "'You shall not murder, you shall not commit adultery, you shall not steal, you shall not give false testimony, honor your father and mother, and love your neighbor as yourself." "All these I have kept," the young man said. "What do I still lack?" Jesus answered, "If you want to be perfect, go, sell your possessions and give to the poor, and you will have treasure in heaven. Then come, follow me." When the young man heard this, he

went away sad, because he had great
wealth (Mark 10:17-22).

When Jesus told the young man to sell all that he
owned, the young man was disappointed. Jesus
loved the man, but the man did not love Jesus
enough to give up his wealth.

Entering the kingdom of God is not without
cost. I was denied a job with a private company
because of my public confession and preaching of
the gospel. I suffered tremendous persecution from
my family and friends because of my decision to
follow Christ. They thought I made a poor decision
in following Christ. But when they saw the favor
and the blessings of God upon my life, they not
only thanked God but decided to believe in the Lord
Jesus.

The citizens of Heaven are the most
privileged citizens in the Universe. The biggest gift
of Heaven to its citizens is eternal life in Christ
Jesus our Lord (Romans 6:23). Eternal life is a gift
only the Almighty God can give. The citizens of
Heaven will inherit "the kingdom prepared for them

since the creation of the world" (Matthew 25:34). Eternal life is inseparable from the kingdom of God. There is no eternal life outside the kingdom of God.

No other kingdom offers eternal life to its citizens; therefore, heavenly citizenship is the most important citizenship in the universe. The citizens of Heaven are also entitled to physical healing, inner peace, personal security, and freedom from fear.

Your earthly citizenship ends one day— either you go to the Lord or the earth will be destroyed altogether. The kingdom of God is the most sustainable government in the universe. As a sustainable government, the kingdom of God can thrive throughout various seasons and changes. No earthy government is sustainable. They may be stable for a time, but they will succumb someday. They will hit by natural disasters, economic calamities, political upheavals or conflicts. Their future is uncertain. They can never guarantee a better life for the future.

The kingdom God is all about the king's affection and care for his people. Nothing comes before the wellbeing of his people. As Deuteronomy 7:6 says, "For you are a people holy to the Lord your God. The Lord your God has chosen you out of all the peoples on the face of the earth to be his people, his treasured possession."

King Jesus gave his life for those who enter his kingdom. His love for us is unconditional. In John 15:13, Jesus said, "Greater love has no one than this: to lay down one's life for one's friends." He did not love us because of our good or bad performance. His love never changes because of our circumstances. If we make mistakes, he still loves us. Even if we wander away from him, he loves us with the same measure of divine love. The love of God is ever present. The parable of the prodigal son confirms this unfailing love that God has for his children.

Paul reassures us that
"neither death, nor life, nor angels, nor principalities, nor powers, nor

things present, nor things to come, nor height, nor depth, nor any other creature, shall be able to separate us from the love of God, which is in Christ Jesus our Lord" (Romans 8:38-39).

God not only loves us, but His love also lives within us. His kingdom is also the place where He is loved first by His people. Nothing should come before the king. As it is written in Matthew 22:37, "Love the Lord your God with all your heart and with all your soul and with all your mind."

Experiencing the Kingdom of God

The kingdom of God is not a theory, theology, or some kind of religious doctrine. The kingdom of God first brings inward changes to a person's life. Jesus said, "Behold, the kingdom of God is within you" (Luke 17:21).

First, saying "the kingdom of God is within you" means that King Jesus is reigning in your life through the power of the Holy Spirit. Jesus lives within you. He is in control of your life. All sorts of storms within your life vanish as Jesus takes precedence over your life. Drugs will no longer ruin your life; the devil will no longer harass you; sin no longer keeps you in captivity. A victorious life is guaranteed when you come under the new management of King Jesus.

In the kingdom of God you are internally and externally secure. Internally, God protects our hearts and minds from harm. Jesus said, "Do not let your hearts be troubled. You believe in God; believe also in me" (John 14:1). Paul's words in Philippians 4:7 are applicable again. Externally, God protects you from physical harm. Jesus said, "But not a hair of your head will perish" (Luke 21:18). So, we have all-rounded protection from God.

Second, the kingdom of God living within you means that you will experience the benefits of the kingdom of God within yourself. Peace and joy will take over anxiety, depression, and fear. Subsequently, inward experiences of the kingdom of God begin to manifest themselves outwardly whereby people begin to witness marked changes in the person's life because now he exhibits new life and character.

The kingdom of God is within you means that you recognize God is working within you. The kingdom of God rules over your heart. You recognize him internally; His presence starts to grow from within. Religion gives external recognition, but the kingdom of God changes you internally. You know God lives within you, and you recognize Him because of the joy and peace that overwhelms. "The peace of God, which transcends all understanding, will guard your hearts and your minds in Christ Jesus," Paul wrote in Philippians 4:7. Additionally, "God's love has been poured out into our hearts through the Holy Spirit, who has been given to us" (Romans 5:5).

Chapter Nine

Kingdom Mandate to the Church

The Church is the highest authority representing and advancing the mission of God's kingdom on earth. The church has no higher mandate than to expand the kingdom of God and to make its king known to the world. When the church embraces and proclaims the message of the kingdom of God, the gates of hell cannot prevail against it. Hell represents the kingdom of the devil. The only way a church can have victory over the power of hell is by proclaiming the authoritative message of the kingdom of God.

The apostles of the early Church were given a mandate to invite sinners to enter the kingdom of God. He sent them to preach the kingdom of God (Luke 9.2). Unfortunately, the subject of the kingdom of God has been put on the backburner in many contemporary church pulpits. Jesus Christ came to die a substitutionary death on behalf of mankind; however, the main reason for his coming to the earth was to restore the lost kingdom and reestablish the kingdom of God on earth.

Preaching about the kingdom is every Christian's lifelong task. We all are God's instruments to advance his kingdom on earth. Jesus instructed his disciples across generations to always be preaching the kingdom of God throughout the earth. Jesus said, "And this gospel of the kingdom will be preached in the whole world as a testimony to all nations, and then the end will come" (Matthew 24:14).

God's government will continue to expand its domination on earth until his return through his church. The church must play its vital role in expanding the dominion of the kingdom of God on earth. That is the main mission of the church. Jesus' central mission for coming to earth was to restore the lost kingdom of God on earth back to its original governor: mankind. Jesus restored the authority Adam lost on earth back to His church. Jesus said, "Do not be afraid, little flock, for your Father has been pleased to give you the kingdom" (Luke

12:32). In giving His kingdom to the church, God literally gave the same governmental authority Jesus had to drive out demons and heal the sick to the church (Mark 16:17-18). The church of Jesus Christ must know how to take its rightful position in the world. Jesus said, "I tell you that you are Peter, and on this rock I will build my church, and the gates of Hades will not overcome it" (Matthew 16:18). You are a rock, which means you are strong; you are not fluid or jelly. You need to maintain your position in Christ. You cannot be moved or pushed around by the enemy. You are to crush and destroy the power of the enemy and drive him from his stronghold. The devil cannot simply be allowed to do his regular business of murdering, stealing, and destroying others while the church has full authority to stop him from doing his carnage. The devil belongs under our feet not in our head. The scripture affirms that the God of peace will soon crush Satan under your feet (Romans 16:20).

Some years back, I went to visit my siblings in Addis Ababa, Ethiopia. They were in the middle of practicing the traditional idol worship when I arrived at their house. A witchdoctor, barely visible because of incense smoke, was sitting in the middle of the room doing his ritual, which involved praising, singing, and at times groaning and screaming. I sat down in the corner of the room and began watching all his activities. Moments later, the witchdoctor said, "The spirit cannot fully manifest because somebody he does not like is in the house." The witchdoctor demanded that person should leave. Unsurprisingly, the person the witchdoctor's spirit had issue with was me. The witchcraft spirit did not like me because of the presence of the Spirit of God. The devil knows that the same anointing that was on Jesus is upon his children. We are Jesus' hands and feet on the earth, we are Christ's ambassadors, and we represent God's interests on earth.

The witchdoctor pointed his finger at me and said, "You must leave the house now." I told the spirit in the witchdoctor, "You devil, it is you who is going to leave! I was raised in this house;

this place belongs to me, not you." I felt the power of God blanket me. I stood up and commanded the witchcraft spirit to leave the house in the name of Jesus Christ of Nazareth.

The witchdoctor fled from the house. My siblings were utterly shocked to see Jesus' victory over the devil and the host of the traditional worship service accepted Christ as her savior that day. Praise the Lord! The devil recognizes the anointing upon God's people and cannot do business as usual in the presence of the anointing of God.

The Church is not a political or humanitarian institution. The church is a spiritual superpower with heavenly authority to serve as a policeman on earth. None of the earthly governments can keep the activities of the devil in check. Their weapons of mass destruction cannot keep the devil at bay. The devil is not afraid of nuclear weapons. His warfare is not of this world. Paul said, "For our struggle is not against flesh and blood, but against the rulers, against the authorities, against the powers of this dark world and against the spiritual forces of evil in the heavenly realms" (Ephesians 6:12). We need to battle the spiritual forces with appropriate weapons. The apostle Paul tells us in Ephesians 6:30 to put on the full armor of God so that when the day of evil comes, we may be able to stand our ground. As Paul writes, the full armor of God includes,

> the belt of truth buckled around your waist, with the breastplate of righteousness in place, and with your feet fitted with the readiness that comes from the gospel of peace. In addition to all this, take up the shield of faith, with which you can extinguish all the flaming arrows of the evil one. Take the helmet of salvation and the sword of the Spirit, which is the word of God (Ephesians 6:14-17).

Many in religious and political circles thought that Jesus came on a political mission. For example, King Herod was "deeply disturbed" when he heard about the birth of Jesus (Matthew 2:1-3). Herod was furious and gave orders to "kill all the boys in Bethlehem and its vicinity who were two-years-old and under, in accordance with the time he had learned from the Magi" (Matthew 2:16). Herod feared another king was being born to take over his throne. But Jesus did not come to establish a secular kingdom. He came to reinstitute the lost kingdom of God on earth.

Jesus' disciples also thought that he had come to bring political independence to the people of Israel, who were under the colonial authority of the Romans. In Acts 1:6, they gather around him and ask, "Lord, are you at this time going to restore the kingdom to Israel?" Nonetheless, Jesus never lost focus in talking about his kingdom at every available opportunity. For example, in John 18:36, Jesus says to Pilate after a long silence, "My kingdom is not of this world. If it were, my servants would fight to prevent my arrest by the Jewish leaders. But now my kingdom is from another place."

Embassy of the Kingdom of God

Each country on earth has an official presence in foreign countries by means of its embassy. The embassy is a governmental institution which is physically established in a foreign country to serve, represent, and protect the interest of the sending country. Embassies are considered part of the extended territory and sovereignty of the sending country in the foreign land. In other words, embassies are considered to be a part of the territory of the home country even though they may be located thousands of miles away. Embassies are inviolable. No authority from the host country is allowed to enter the embassy premises without permission from the embassy itself.

Official embassy business is executed by an ambassador who is appointed as chief diplomat by his home government, Monarch, President or Prime Minister. An ambassador always identifies himself with his country. He is a citizen of the sending country; he speaks its language; he is a spokesperson for his country. In his or her capacity as a spokesperson, the ambassador introduces and educates the people of the host land about his country.

The ambassador is in constant communication with the home government. He receives instructions from the home government on how best to serve and protect the interests of the country in that foreign land. The ambassador is not expected to serve his personal interests while he is representing his home country in the foreign land. He or she is fully dedicated to serve the missions which have been entrusted to him or her by the home government. The home country's interests come before his/her personal interests; the ambassador's main purpose is to advance the interest of his/her country at any cost.

Even though an ambassador lives in a foreign country, he/she is not subjected to the rules and cultures of the host country. Ambassadors are protected by diplomatic immunity as long as they live in the foreign land. For example, an ambassador cannot be subject to fines for traffic violations while driving in the host country. An ambassador can park his car in a "no-parking zone" at any time, and his car can neither be seized nor towed. An ambassador's luggage and personal belongings are not subject to search even during international flights.

The Church of Jesus Christ is the embassy of the kingdom of God on earth. Its purpose is to represent and advance the interests of the kingdom of God on earth. Adam was appointed ambassador of the kingdom of God on earth until he lost his authority to the devil. Then, God sent His son to restore the lost kingdom of God after the fall of Adam, in which the devil took over man's dominion over earth through treachery and deception. For thousands of years, earth fell under the dominion of Satan, but Jesus came to force Satan out from his illegitimate rise to power on earth. Jesus took Satan's authority and gave it to his church, saying to Peter, "On this rock I will build my church, and the gates of Hades will not overcome it" (Matthew

16:18). Even demons cried out to Jesus, "Have you come to destroy us?" (Mark 1:24).

The Church is an embassy of the kingdom of God on earth, which has forcefully reclaimed the lost kingdom under the divine authority of God. Jesus had to first establish His church (embassy) on earth before he could appoint ambassadors. After he established his church, Jesus appointed ambassadors as apostles, prophets, evangelists, pastors, teachers, and administrators to represent the kingdom of God on earth. Paul declared himself an ambassador in Ephesians 6:20. All believers are fully-accredited ambassadors of the kingdom of God, mandated to serve in the Church of Jesus Christ on earth. As the apostle Paul reminds us, "We are therefore Christ's ambassadors, as though God were making his appeal through us. We implore you on Christ's behalf: Be reconciled to God" (2 Corinthians 5:20). As ambassadors of Christ, we have been mandated to represent his kingdom, to expand it, and to serve the citizens of the kingdom of God in a foreign world. Jesus commissioned his disciples to "go and make disciples of all nations, baptizing them in the name of the Father and of the Son and of the Holy Spirit, and teaching them to obey everything I have commanded you. And surely I am with you always, to the very end of the age" (Matthew 28:18-20).

We are foreigners and strangers on this earth. This world is not our permanent home. Jesus said "They are not of the world, even as I am not of it" (John 17:16). Our citizenship is in heaven. The world is our place of assignment to do the mission of the kingdom of God on earth until we depart from here.

Believers are spread across the earth to expand the kingdom of God. Some of us are ambassadors to our neighbors, while others are ambassadors in business, professional, and religious settings. It is as Paul says "We are therefore Christ's ambassadors, as though God were making his appeal through us. We implore you on Christ's behalf: Be reconciled to God" (2 Corinthians 5:20).

Chapter Ten

Seek First His Righteousness

Matthew 6:33 reads, "but seek first his righteousness, and all these things will be given to you as well." The Hebrew word for righteousness is *sedaqah* which means to have right standing or to observe or conform to the rule of God. As citizens of earth, we are required to have right standing according to the laws of our country. A person not having right standing with the laws of one's country is a criminal or delinquent.

Jesus emphasized that the most important thing in life is to have right standing with God. Therefore, one should give a high priority to have right standing with God. However, God's righteousness cannot be attained through one's efforts. In Isaiah 64:6, we are told that our righteous deeds are but filthy rags before God. One may appear to be morally upright person before men, but in God's sight we all are but wretched sinners. As Romans 3:10 states, "there is no one who is righteous, not even one." Our sins prevent us from having right standing with God. Sin is lawlessness in the sight of God (1 John 3:4). We have lost right standing with God due to our sinful nature.

However, God made a way for us to have right standing with Him by sending His only begotten son to shed his blood on the cross. In Hebrews 10:11 we read that "We have confidence to enter the Most Holy Place by the blood of Jesus." The shed blood of Jesus is the only way for us to obtain right standing with God. The blood of Jesus was shed on the cross of Calvary to cleanse us from our sins (1 John 1:7). The scripture tells us that "If we confess our sins, he is faithful and just to forgive us our sins and to purify us from all unrighteousness (1 John 1:9). The main mission of Jesus was to reestablish our right standing with God within the kingdom of God.

Christ is the way to obtain the righteousness of God. We cannot receive righteousness without seeking Christ first. Therefore, righteousness comes through faith in Christ. God's righteousness is not something we can earn. As Romans 5:17 declares,

"God's abundant provision of grace and of the gift of righteousness reign in life through the one man, Jesus Christ!" God bestowed his unmerited righteousness upon us through Jesus Christ because of his love and kindness. "For God so loved the world that he gave his one and only Son, that whoever believes in him shall not perish but have eternal life (John 3:16). God's righteousness is granted as an act of God's goodness and kindness to save and deliver mankind. Therefore, we cannot earn or deserve God's righteousness.

Jesus is our righteousness, and his righteousness is transferred through faith in Jesus Christ to all who believe in him (Romans 3:22). Righteousness is bestowed upon us the moment we believe in him. It is not something that comes gradually once we first believe in Christ. We became partakers in the righteousness of God as His free gift. We do not contribute anything towards our new righteousness. For example, Abraham "believed God, and it was credited to him as righteousness" (Genesis 15:6). Understand then that those who have this faith are the children of Abraham. The Scriptures foresaw that God would justify the Gentiles by faith and announced the Gospel in advance to Abraham: "All nations will be blessed through you" (Genesis 22:18). So those who rely on faith are blessed along with Abraham, the man of faith. Indeed, if righteousness could be obtained through the law, Christ died for nothing (Galatians 2:21). Jesus came to fulfill all righteousness. He was the only human being who could fulfill all righteousness for he was the only sinless person who could satisfy God's requirements. Jesus provided it for us. When we enter the kingdom of Christ through the repentance of our sins, he clothes us with his garment for righteousness and leads us in the path of righteousness all days of our life.

But we must desire this right standing to receive it. Jesus said, "blessed are those who hunger and thirst for righteousness, for they will be filled" (Mathew 5.6). Jesus wanted us to receive his righteousness before anything else. Therefore, to be right with God should be our utmost desire. We should seek right standing with God before anything else. The trouble comes when we seek other things more than such righteousness of God. God extended his righteousness to all humanity through Jesus Christ. God does not show favoritism based on race, culture, color, economic background or gender. Once we receive the righteousness of God, we need to walk within it. We should maintain the righteousness of God by being saturated in the Word of God. All Scripture is God-breathed and is useful for teaching, rebuking, correcting and training in righteousness (2 Timothy 3:16).

Nothing is more important than having right standing with God as God's righteousness restores physical and spiritual blessing to our lives. When we have right standing with God, we will have salvation which is the gift of eternal life. If we have right standing with God, we are protected and directed by God. The Lord says, "I will rescue him; I will protect him, for he acknowledges my name (Psalm 91:14).

The righteousness of God brings wholesome peace and health to our spiritual and physical body. The scripture declares that,

> "The righteous (a person with right standing with God) will flourish like a palm tree, they will grow like a cedar of Lebanon; planted in the house of the Lord, they will flourish in the courts of our God. They will still bear fruit in old age, they will stay fresh and green" (Psalm 92:12-14).

The life of a righteous man is life full of strength, longevity, and fruitfulness. The scripture declares, "with long life I will satisfy him" (Psalm 91:16).

Equally important is knowing that those who seek the righteousness of God will suffer persecution. As the Lord Jesus said, "blessed are those who are persecuted because of righteousness, for theirs is the kingdom of heaven (Mathew 5.10). The world mounts opposition against those who reject its ways. For example, when you lose your longtime friendship in order to have fellowship with

God, your friends will begin to treat you differently. They will label you as a strange or insane. When you quit night clubs or bad habits for church or fellowship with church people, your friends will no longer want to be around you. When you cancel going to games in order to have time with the Lord in prayer, you will lose those longtime friends or even your family. Similarly, God grants us salvation, deliverance and healing when we establish our relationship with him and remain with him. In fact, there is no salvation, without having right relationship with God. There is no deliverance without having a relationship with God. There is no healing without having a relationship with God.

God's righteousness protects the righteous from the attack of the enemy. The scriptures affirm that

> He will save you from the fowler's snare and from the deadly pestilence. He will cover you with his feathers, and under his wings you will find refuge; his faithfulness will be your shield and rampart. You will not fear the terror of night, nor the arrow that flies by day, nor the pestilence that

stalks in the darkness, nor the plague that destroys at midday. A thousand may fall at your side, ten thousand at your right hand, but it will not come near you. You will only observe with your eyes and see the punishment of the wicked (Psalms 91:4-8).

The most successful person on the planet is the one who is in right standing with God. The most important relationship in the world is our relationship with God. No relationship is as important as our relationship with God. Every other relationship in our lives is temporary but our relationship with God is eternal. Therefore, we should pursue to have right standing with God all the time.

Chapter Eleven

The Kingdom of Joy

In Romans 14:17, we read, "For the kingdom of God is not a matter of eating and drinking, but of righteousness, peace and *joy* in the Holy Spirit." Joy means deep pleasure or satisfaction with God. The source of divine joy in the kingdom of God is the King himself. Jesus was full of joy because he was anointed with the oil of joy, which is mentioned in Psalm 45:7: "Therefore God, your God, has set you above your companions by anointing you with the oil of joy" (Luke 10:21). Jesus was full of joy through the Holy Spirit. He received divine joy from the Holy Spirit and was thus the most joyful person on earth. Jesus was also the most pursued person on earth because he had something that no one else had. To be with Jesus means to be exposed to his joy.

Jesus came to give us joy. The angel said to them, "Do not be afraid. I bring you good news that will cause great joy for all the people. Today in the town of David a Savior has been born to you; he is the Messiah, the Lord" (Luke 2.10-11). Many people came to Jesus with so many kinds of brokenness, and he gave them his joy by healing their physical infirmities. As is written in Matthew 15:30, "Great crowds came to him, bringing the lame, the blind, the crippled, the mute and many others, and laid them at his feet; and he healed them." God shared His joy with humanity through Jesus. Philip, for example, went to the city of Samaria and told the people there about the Messiah.

> Crowds listened intently to Philip because they were eager to hear his message and see the miraculous signs he did. Many evil spirits were cast out, screaming as they left their victims. And many who had been paralyzed or lame were healed. So there was great joy in that city (Acts 8:5-8).

The Ethiopian official went rejoicing after accepting Jesus into his life.

> So beginning with this same Scripture, Philip told him the Good News about Jesus. As they rode

along, they came to some water, and the eunuch said, "Look! There's some water! Why can't I be baptized?" He ordered the carriage to stop, and they went down into the water, and Philip baptized him. When they came up out of the water, the Spirit of the Lord snatched Philip away. The eunuch never saw him again but went on his way rejoicing (Acts 8:35-39 NLT).

If we remain with Jesus in his kingdom, we will enjoy the joy Jesus himself had. He tells us this in John 15:11: "I have told you this so that my joy may be in you and that your joy may be complete." One of the things we experience upon encountering Jesus is his extraordinary joy. I remember when I had a visit from Jesus in 2011. The moment Jesus came and started talking with me, unspeakable joy flooded the gates of my heart. Where the joy of the Lord is present, anxiety and depression disappear.

One of the privileges we get when we are admitted to the kingdom of God is receiving His joy. In Luke 10:20, Jesus says, "Rejoice that your names are written in heaven." He tells us to rejoice for being allowed to enter the kingdom of God, for outside of the kingdom, the joy of God cannot be attained. We cannot gain the joy of the Lord through our material possessions or professional aid such as psychological and medical interventions—only God can give us inner joy. To receive this, we must first be admitted to the kingdom of God.

The joy of the Lord cannot be interrupted by difficult circumstances such as financial, health, social, or other personal crises. Hebrews 12:2 reveals that Jesus had joy even while was suffering on the cross: "For the joy set before him he endured the cross, scorning its shame, and sat down at the right hand of the throne of God."

The apostle Paul had joy in the midst of trials. He said, "in all our troubles my joy knows no bounds" (2 Corinthians 7:2). Paul wrote about the Macedonian churches that they had overflowing joy in the midst of a very severe trial (2 Corinthians 8:2). James implores us to "consider it pure joy, my brothers and sisters, whenever you face trials of many kinds" (James 1:2). The apostle Peter wrote that trials and persecutions cannot derail the joy of the Lord. In 1 Peter 1:6, it is written: "In all this you greatly rejoice, though now for a little while you may have had to suffer grief in all kinds of trials."

Jesus never promised a temptation or trial-free kingdom until it is fully realized, but Jesus did promise that we will have his static joy through difficult circumstances. The joy of the Lord is a constant flow if we always remain in his kingdom.

We could be experiencing financial stress, confined to a hospital bed, or undergoing other personal troubles, but the joy in our heart cannot be disrupted. I once heard the true story of two patients who shared a hospital room for a while. One patient had his bed by the window and the other bed had no window. The patient by the window would tell the other patient about the colorful flowers, stunning landscapes, and other beautiful things he was seeing through the window. He told the other patient about his magnificent view every day until his unexpected death.

Subsequently, the other patient asked the nurses if he could be moved near the window to have that beautiful outside view. However, the nurses responded, "There are no attractive things to see outside. If you look outside, you will only see dirty streets and homeless people roaming around." The patient responded, "The other patient was telling me about the beautiful things outside." The nurses revealed that the man was blind and there was no way he could see that. However, they did not understand that even though the late patient had no physical sight, his spiritual eyes were opened. The Lord was giving him a tour of heaven every day on his death bed before he ultimately went to heaven. This is a clear example of the overflowing joy of the Lord amid incomprehensible pain and suffering. Jesus said, "Come to me, all you who are weary and burdened, and I will give you rest" (Matthew 11:28). For those who choose to enter the kingdom, Jesus will lift off burdens and pour out his joy. These people whose burdens are lifted will be the most joyful. Jesus says in John 17:13 that those who follow him will have the full measure of his joy within themselves. 1 Thessalonians 5:16-18 reminds us to "Rejoice always, pray continually, give thanks in all circumstances; for this is God's will for you in Christ Jesus."

Chapter Twelve

The Kingdom of Peace

"For the kingdom of God is not a matter of eating and drinking, but of righteousness, *peace* and joy in the Holy Spirit," Romans 14:17 reads. As is revealed in this verse, the kingdom of God is a kingdom of peace. Nothing disturbs the peace in the kingdom of God.

Peace can be defined as an absence of disturbances, fear, and violence. Peace is one of the fundamental human needs. Lack of peace not only affects personal and community life but it affects animal and plant communities as well. For example, animals have been forced out of their environment because of armed conflicts. As a professor of peace studies for many years, I wrote an academic textbook as well as many articles on the subject of peace, including an academic textbook and many journal articles. One of my textbooks, *Promoting Collective Security in Africa: The Roles and Responsibilities of the United Nations, African States and Western Powers*, was the product of many years of scholarly work in the field of peace studies. In all my studies, I indicate that peace is a fundamental human rights.

In the secular or worldly context, peace can be divided into negative and positive peace. Negative peace refers to having a superficial peace with oneself and with others. The state of peace is shallow. The absence of war does not necessarily mean there is peace. It may appear peaceful externally, but internally it is miserable. Outwardly, people may smile, but their heart is full of heaviness, depression, anxiety and fear. They pretend to be happy by covering up their true feelings. They may look peaceful early in the day but may end up committing suicide later in the day. Those with negative peace are not open to professional help, even though they know they need it.

Positive peace, on the other hand, refers to having a more stable internal peace even though it may not be sustainable. People are transparent about their lack of peace at the personal level or in their relations with others. Furthermore, they are also motivated to take positive steps to tackle the underlining problems causing the lack of personal peace and bad relationships with others. They are willing to receive medical and professional help, such as third-party mediation and negotiation to restore durable peace with themselves and others. However, positive peace lasts only as long as the other parties in a relationship show an equal levels of commitment to keeping the peace. If one party walks away from the peace agreement, the peace treaty will fail. Therefore, positive peace relies on the constant commitment of all parties, and it can only be sustained if each party adhering to the terms of the peace agreement.

A third kind of peace is what we call Divine Peace, which originates from God himself. Jesus said, "Peace I leave with you; my peace I give you. I do not give to you as the world gives" (John 14:27). As we discussed, the two kinds of worldly peace—negative and positive peace—are contingent upon individual efforts. But the peace that Jesus gives is not dependent upon human efforts. Jesus himself is the source of peace. "For he himself is our peace" (Ephesians 2:14). Jesus is called the "Prince of Peace" in Isaiah 9:6. Jesus said, "I have told you these things, so that in me you may have peace" (John 16:33). Jesus delivered his peace to the disciples through the Holy Spirit. John 20:22 recounts that Jesus breathed on them and said, "Receive the Holy Spirit." The only way to receive divine peace is by entering into the kingdom of God, which is not one "of eating and drinking, but of righteousness, peace and joy in the Holy Spirit" (Romans 14:17).

Divine peace is not dependent upon our internal or external circumstances. It is an unconditional peace. Paul described divine peace in Philippians 4:7, saying that "the peace of God, which transcends all understanding, will guard your hearts and your minds in Christ Jesus." Divine peace is not found in religion, but it saturates in the kingdom of Christ, and those who are outside of the kingdom will not experience it. There are so many

Christians who have committed suicide, gotten divorced, mutilated their bodies, or became addicted to drugs and alcohol in search of peace. However, divine peace cannot be found outside the kingdom of God. The moment we enter the kingdom of God, the peace of God begins to reign in our heart. Divine peace is permanent.

The Bible says,

> On the evening of that first day of the week, when the disciples were together, with the doors locked for fear of the Jewish leaders, Jesus came and stood among them and said, Peace be with you! After he said this, he showed them his hands and side. The disciples were overjoyed when they saw the Lord. Again Jesus said, 'Peace be with you! (John 20:19-20).

No door that is shut or any walls or fences shall block the peace of Christ. Jesus brings his peace by breaking down all obstacles that stand in his way. Nothing stands in the way of the peace of Christ.

Divine peace originates only from God Himself. Jesus declared in John 14:27 that the peace he gives us is not from this world; it is heavenly in nature. It brings inner peace, and external factors such as a failing economy, clashing politics, or a deteriorating social relations cannot dictate your inner peace. You will not fear the future because you will live with a sense of peace, calm, and stability, both spiritually and emotionally. Your past will not intimidate you. The enemy cannot disturb you because God has given you authority over the enemy. Your peace is not dependent on the type of car you drive, the kind of house or neighborhood in which you live, or the kind of work you have. No situation or circumstance takes divine peace away from you. As a citizen of the kingdom of God, you enjoy peace in the midst of chaos, pain, and upheavals.

Jesus said to the fearful and intimidated disciples, "Peace unto you" (John 20:19-21). God's peace cannot be affected by how much the world may hate us. The peace of God persists through the attacks of hate, persecution, and sickness; it is not dependent upon circumstances. God acts independently of circumstances. You may be in a prison, but the peace of God can reach you over your agony, misery, guilt, and loneliness. You may be in a hospital bed, but his peace can find you. You are never far from the peace of God, for the kingdom of God brings overwhelming peace despite satanic attacks or one's personal shortcomings.

Chapter Thirteen

The Kingdom of Mercy

Mercy is the pardoning of sin, not promoting injustice. When justice overlooks crime, it's mercy. God never justified sin through granting of mercy. God does not overlook our sins. He punished sin with the full force of justice through the sacrifice of Jesus. It is true that God is love and that He acts in a loving way, but He also acts with justice. He is a just judge. If God was not just, He could have saved Jesus from the cross. But when it came to punishing sin, it did not matter that Jesus was the son of God. Jesus paid the full price necessary to set us free from the penalty of death. As such, he was the atonement for our sins.

Thus, we cannot depend on our good deeds as the basis for our salvation. Jesus restored our relationship with the Father through his substitutionary death. We not only gained forgiveness for our sins through Christ, but we were also reunited with our heavenly Father. We became a family member with God all over again. We are accepted by God because Jesus met all the requirements of the Father. The devil can no longer hold us hostage because Christ paid in full the price our sin. The devil can no longer hold us for our sins because Christ stepped in on our behalf and paid the cost of our sins in full. We are therefore entitled to the "unmerited favor" of God through Christ.

The story of the prodigal son in Luke 15 represents the mercy of God extended into those who come to the kingdom of God. In the story we find a father and his two sons. The father represents God. The sons represent God's people. All seems to be perfect until one son comes up with the idea of taking his share of his inheritance and going away on his own. We read that younger son takes his share and wastes it through wild living in a far-away country. After a while, he faces the life-threatening consequences. He began to starve and becomes unable to fulfill his basic needs. He finally decides to return to his father, even if his father may not receive him as a son, but as a servant. So he got up and went back to his father. "But while he was still a long way off, his father saw him and was filled with compassion for him; he ran to his son, threw his arms around him and kissed him" (Luke 15:20).

We notice that the depth of the father's love was amazing! The father does not waste a single second looking back on the mistakes of his wayward son. He quickly loved him all the more. The parable continues:

> "The father said to his servants, 'Quick! Bring the best robe and put it on him. Put a ring on his finger and sandals on his feet. Bring the fattened calf and kill it. Let's have a feast and celebrate. For this son of mine was dead and is alive again; he was lost and is found.' So they began to celebrate" (Luke 15:22-25).

This is a typical example of God's unconditional mercy for the one who does not deserve it at all. God always grants His mercy to whoever asks for it.

We must understand that there is no safer or fulfilling place than the kingdom of God. The younger son did not appreciate the privileges he had

had in his father's house until he left it. So many believers have run away from the presence of God but cannot make it back again. Some people's lives end tragically. Some spend the best part of their life in prison. Some are addicted to drugs and cannot break away from them. Some become mentally or physically debilitated because they departed from the love and care of our heavenly Father.

Many important lessons can be drawn from the actions of the lost son. To begin with, he knew his father's wealth and potential. He recognized that he was born of a rich father. So many Christians do not think of their heavenly father as rich. Secondly, he knew that he had a share of his father's wealth. Some Christians do not think they have a fair share as a child of God. Thirdly, the younger son admitted that he had made a mistake and was prepared to ask for forgiveness. Many Christians find it hard to admit their mistakes and to reconcile with God. Fourth, he knew that his father loved him and forgave him every time he made mistake. We should know that our father in heaven is a forgiving

God. He never runs out of mercy. He is always willing to forgive if we sincerely look to Him for it.

Fifth, the son knew that his father's house was the wealthiest place there could be! Not many people outside of the kingdom of God realize that we are having fun in the kingdom!

When I decided to accept Christ as my Lord and Savior at the age of nineteen, many of my friends thought I had locked myself into a prison cell. They failed to realize that life in the house of God is wonderfully pleasant, entertaining, and vibrant. In the parable of the prodigal son, the father put up a party to celebrate the return of his lost son. God the Father stretches out His arms to receive us.

The devil tries to misrepresent God to us. He tells us that God does not love us anymore, but the devil is nothing but a liar. Once God forgives our sins, he also forgets them. The intense love of the Father is waiting for us. As the Scripture says, "the righteous will shine like the sun in the kingdom of their Father" (Matthew 13:43). The house of God is the most fun place in this universe. It is not the end of the world, as devil tries to present it. It is the beginning of a new and joyful life.

There are countless people who run away from the kingdom of God in pursuit of pleasure but become entangled in deadly addictions, afflicted with incurable diseases, subjected to physical abuse and mental torment, thrown in prison, and suffering a premature death. Life outside the kingdom of God is terrible! Some parents think it is normal for their teenagers to experience an ungodly lifestyles, but I must say that they expose their kids to demons and some of their offspring never pull through.

Useful lessons may be drawn from the life of the older son as well. Firstly, he faithfully lived in the house of his father. He never thought of a life beyond of his father's protection. As a result, he lived safe and secure life all his life. Secondly, he was continuously faithful to his father. He was working but did not enjoy it. Third, he was obedient to his father. Not one time was his father disappointed in him for disobedience. But he never took advantage of his rights and privileges as a child in his father's house; therefore, he never enjoyed anything. He was not much better off than the servants. Some of the servants even enjoyed their privileges more than he did.

Some believers are like the older brother who only spend their years in the house of God and do not enjoy the privileges God has or them. The younger believers make up for lost time and enjoy the benefits of the kingdom. They can be easily filled with the Holy Ghost or receive healing simply because they appreciate God more than older believers. Jesus said that the last shall become first and the first become last (Matthew 20:16).

Fourthly, the older brother was an angry fellow. This is exemplified in his reaction when his younger returned in Luke 15:28-32:

> The older brother became angry and refused to go in. So his father went out and pleaded with him. But he answered his father, "Look! All these years I've been slaving for you and never disobeyed your orders. Yet you never gave me even a young goat so I could celebrate with my friends. But when this son of yours

who has squandered your property with prostitutes comes home, you kill the fattened calf for him!" "My son," the father said, "you are always with me, and everything I have is yours. But we had to celebrate and be glad, because this brother of yours was dead and is alive again; he was lost and is found."

The older brother was angry with himself, his father, and his brother. He was angry about everything!

There are so many angry Christians. They are mad at their good Father for no reason, and they lack appreciation for what they have in the house of God. They are upset with their family, co-workers in ministry, or even themselves. But anger never helps anything, and it cannot be God's fault.

Fifthly, the older son was full of complaints. He complained to himself for obeying and serving in the house of his father for all that time. Do you know that God does not appreciate ungratefulness? Do you remember how God punished Miriam for complaining about Moses? God also punished those who complained about Him and his servant Moses. Complaining only brings judgment, whereas thanksgiving in every circumstance brings God's blessings upon our lives. Paul and Silas had all good reason to complain when they were in the Athenian prison. But despite severe beating, they sang hymns and praised until the Lord responded with a mighty shaking in the prison.

Just as the older son was ignorant of his rights and privileges as a child of a wealthy father, so some believers do not know of the privileges they have in the kingdom of God. The older son lived on a low-level; he never utilized the wealth, the royal clothes or entertained in his father's house. Some of us do not appreciate the privileges we have in the kingdom of God.

Some new believers come from behind and enjoy the privileges of the kingdom more than older brothers and sisters. Many older Christians become bitter when new believers begin enjoying the privileges of the kingdom more than themselves. Too many older Christians have been just following traditions, practicing religion, and "playing" church, but not fully experiencing the excitement of the kingdom of God. The church is supposed to be God's embassy on earth and delivering the privileges of Christ to its citizens and blessing the world. So many Christians fail to understand the abundant life in the kingdom of God. They think it is a secluded, boring, lonely place. The fact of the matter is that they have it wrong. I commend the young brother for knowing what is entitled to him, but getting his share and squandering it recklessly was wrong. Everything we own outside God will one day run out. God is our only unending source of abundant life. He prepared for us a kingdom, and there dwells His abundance for ever and ever.

Chapter Fourteen

The Kingdom of Power

Earthly governments expand their control over new territories through military power. They invade foreign lands and extend their political and economic control over them. Some governments continue to rule the lands they occupied centuries ago; others have lost control of the occupied territories because their power diminished. To keep their rule in the occupied lands, they must maintain superior military power.

Similarly, the kingdom of God came to earth with power. The Lord Jesus said, "the Kingdom of Heaven has been forcefully advancing" (Matthew 11:12, NLT). Jesus faced violent resistance from the forces of evil as soon as he began establishing his kingdom. He was forced to leave cities and exiled to a foreign country; he faced accusations from religious leaders and was questioned by political authorities. He was tempted by Satan and crucified for the cause of the kingdom; however, Jesus overcame all human and spiritual authorities through the power of God and successfully inaugurated the kingdom of God on earth. Jesus was visibly confirmed by the Father and the Holy Spirit before beginning his earthly ministry. Jesus received the power of the Holy Spirit after being baptized in water at the Jordan River. The Scripture says, "As soon as Jesus was baptized, he went up out of the water. At that moment heaven was opened, and he saw the Spirit of God descending like a dove and alighting on him (Matthew 3:16). Jesus had never publicly confronted his enemies until after he received the power of the Holy Spirit. He never taught or preached about his kingdom nor perform miracles prior to that day. However, from that day on, Jesus ministered in the power of the Holy Spirit. The scripture confirms that Jesus entered every city demonstrating the power of the Holy Spirit. For example, Jesus went to Galilee with the power (Luke 4:14).

It was only with the power of the Holy Spirit that Jesus was able to do what he did. The Scripture says, "God anointed Jesus of Nazareth with the

Holy Spirit and power. Then Jesus went around doing good and healing all who were under the power of the devil, because God was with him" (Acts 10:38).

Jesus's healing acts were performed through the power of the Holy Spirit. Luke 5:17 reads, "One day Jesus was teaching, and Pharisees and teachers of the law were sitting there. They had come from every village of Galilee and from Judea and Jerusalem. And the power of the Lord was with Jesus to heal the sick." We also read that power went out of Jesus to heal the woman who suffered from a loss of blood over many years. The woman only touched his robe to connect to the readily available power in Lord Jesus Christ. Mark 5:30-33 recounts this story:

> At once Jesus realized that power had gone out from him. He turned around in the crowd and asked, "Who touched my clothes?" "You see the people crowding against you," his disciples answered, "and yet you can ask, 'Who touched me?'" But Jesus kept looking around to see who had done it. Then the

woman, knowing what had happened to her, came and fell at his feet and, trembling with fear, told him the whole truth. He said to her, "Daughter, your faith has healed you. Go in peace and be freed from your suffering."

Jesus could cast out powerful demons because he was full of the power of the Holy Spirit. Jesus said, "If I drive out demons by the finger of God, then the kingdom of God has come upon you" (Luke 11:20). No powerful demon can withstand the power that is in Jesus.

Matthew 8:28-34 presents the story of Jesus casting out powerful demons from men living among the tomb. The evil spirits were so violent that no one dared to come near the area. They attacked people and hurt them. But when they saw Jesus, they cried out and fell at his feet, crying out, "What do you want with us, Son of God? Have you come here to torture us before the appointed time?" Jesus commanded the unclean spirit to come out of the men. A similar story takes place in Luke 8:26-39.

In all these stories, when the powerful Son of God—full of the power of the Holy Spirit—shows up, the evil spirits lose their power before he said a word; demons must submit to the greater power of God on Jesus Christ. Jesus performed many miracles with this power. He turned water to wine and raised the dead through the power of the Holy Spirit. Jesus walked on the water by the power of God. He calmed the wind by the power of God. He fed 5000 plus by the power of God. Jesus cancelled funerals by the power of God. Jesus entered every household with this power and never negotiated with his opponents. It was with the power of the Holy Spirit that he advanced the kingdom of God.

Jesus instructed his disciples to wait in Jerusalem until they should receive power from the Holy Spirit. He told them, "I am going to send you what my Father has promised; but stay in the city until you have been clothed with power from on high" (Luke 24:49). He reemphasized again the importance of receiving this power in Acts 1:8, which reads, "But you will receive power when the Holy Spirit comes on you; and you will be my witnesses in Jerusalem, and in all Judea and Samaria, and to the ends of the earth." Jesus wanted them to receive their power before they should go from city to city to expand the kingdom of God. The work of God is not mainly done by planning committees, prayer groups or theology classes but by men and women who are anointed with the power of the Holy Spirt.

The disciples received power of the Holy Spirit on the day of Pentecost and went forth from Jerusalem to the uttermost part of the earth. For example, over 8,000 people were saved through the teaching with signs, and wonders performed by the apostles in a short period of time. The religious and political authorities did all that was possible to stop them from spreading the message of the kingdom of God. Among other things, they kicked apostles out of cities, jailed them, beat them, and executed them. However, none of that could stop the apostles. They expanded the kingdom of God to neighboring cities such as Samaria, Joppa, Judea, and Gaza. Furthermore, the message of the Gospel has already crossed into far regions including Africa and Asia, after the Jews from those regions received Jesus as their messiah on the day of Pentecost. Therefore, attempts to stop the apostles from preaching in Jerusalem simply came too late as the message of the Gospel had reached to the larger region before the persecution began in Jerusalem.

The apostles were full of the power of God from the day of Pentecost onwards. Peter was so filled with this power that his shadow could heal the sick. Acts 5:15-16 describes how "people brought the sick into the streets and laid them on beds and mats so that at least Peter's shadow might fall on them as he passed by. Crowds gathered from the towns around Jerusalem, bringing their sick and those tormented by impure spirits, and all of them were healed." Indeed, any cloth that had been in contact with the body of the apostle Paul could heal the sick and cast demons out wherever they went because of the power of God. Acts 19:11-12 proclaims, "God did extraordinary miracles through Paul, so that even handkerchiefs and aprons that had touched him were taken to the sick, and their illnesses were cured and the evil spirits left them."

Paul said his message was full of power, not just by nice religious language. The apostle Paul reaffirmed that the kingdom of God "is not a matter of talk but of power" (1Corinthians 4:20). He explained that the kingdom of God is not focused on eloquent preaching, articulate teaching, or impressive religious oratory. His messages were accompanied by demonstrations of God's power to prove this point (Acts 19:11). In his epistle to the Corinthian believers, Paul writes, "My message and my preaching were not with wise and persuasive words, but with a demonstration of the Spirit's power" (1 Corinthians 2:4).

Paul drove out demons. He healed the sick. He raised the dead. He challenged the political and intellectual authorities of his day. Jesus said, the kingdom of heaven has been subjected to violence, and violent people have been raiding it (Matthew

11:12). The apostles advanced the kingdom of God in a forceful way amid stiff opposition!

The same power of God is available to us today to expand the kingdom of God to include our household, our neighborhood, our city, our country and the world. Jesus delegated similar power to his disciples to expand his kingdom to thier own generation. We also will have the same victory over demonic powers if we operate by the same power of the Holy Spirit. The kingdom God can only be enforced by the power of the Holy Spirit. Amen!

Made in the USA
Monee, IL
18 April 2024

57095263R00085